THE ECOLOGY OF LAW

THE ECOLOGY OF LAW

Toward a Legal System in Tune with Nature and Community

FRITJOF CAPRA
and UGO MATTEI

Berrett–Koehler Publishers, Inc.
a BK Currents book

BERRETT-KOEHLER PUBLISHERS, INC.
1333 Broadway, Suite 1000
Oakland, CA 94612-1921
Tel: (510) 817-2277   Fax: (510) 817-2278   www.bkconnection.com

ORDERING INFORMATION
Quantity sales. Special discounts are available on quantity purchases by corporations, associations, and others. For details, contact the "Special Sales Department" at the Berrett-Koehler address above.

Individual sales. Berrett-Koehler publications are available through most bookstores. They can also be ordered directly from Berrett-Koehler: Tel: (800) 929-2929; Fax: (802) 864-7626; www.bkconnection.com

Orders for college textbook/course adoption use. Please contact Berrett-Koehler: Tel: (800) 929-2929; Fax: (802) 864-7626.

Orders by U.S. trade bookstores and wholesalers. Please contact Ingram Publisher Services, Tel: (800) 509-4887; Fax: (800) 838-1149; E-mail: customer.service@ingrampublisher services.com; or visit www.ingrampublisherservices.com/Ordering for details about electronic ordering.

Berrett-Koehler and the BK logo are registered trademarks of Berrett-Koehler Publishers, Inc.

Printed in the United States of America

Berrett-Koehler books are printed on long-lasting acid-free paper. When it is available, we choose paper that has been manufactured by environmentally responsible processes. These may include using trees grown in sustainable forests, incorporating recycled paper, minimizing chlorine in bleaching, or recycling the energy produced at the paper mill.

Produced by Wilsted & Taylor Publishing Services
Copyediting Nancy Evans *Design* Yvonne Tsang *Index* Derek Gottlieb

LIBRARY OF CONGRESS CATALOGING-IN-PUBLICATION DATA
Capra, Fritjof, author.
  The ecology of law : toward a legal system in tune with nature and community / Fritjof Capra and Ugo Mattei. — First edition.
      pages cm
   Includes bibliographical references and index.
   ISBN 978-1-62656-206-6 (hardcover)
1. Science and law. 2. Environmental law. I. Mattei, Ugo. II. Title.

K487.S3C37 2015

340'.1—dc23   2015021650

First Edition

20 19 18 17 16 15   10 9 8 7 6 5 4 3 2 1

*To all the bright young people
worldwide who pursue an
academic education still hoping
to change the world.*

Contents

Preface

Over the last four decades, dozens of scholarly and popular books have explored the fundamental change of worldview, or change of paradigms, that is now occurring in science and in society—a change from a mechanistic to a holistic and ecological vision of reality. None of these books, however, has paid attention to the fact that this paradigm shift has an important legal dimension. This legal dimension is the central focus of *The Ecology of Law*.

The idea for this book originated in a series of conversations between a scientist (Capra) and a legal scholar (Mattei) about the concept of law in science and jurisprudence. The first conversations took place on a tennis court; they led to more structured discussions and subsequently to two semester-long seminars we taught at the University of California Hastings College of the Law in San Francisco. As our fascination with the subject grew, we decided to turn our discussions into a book.

When people think about law, they usually think about lawyers and their court cases. *The Ecology of Law* is the first book to present the law as a system of knowledge and jurisprudence—the theory and philosophy of law—and as an intellectual discipline with a history and conceptual structure that show surprising parallels to those of natural science. Indeed, the two disciplines have interacted throughout history; as they have coevolved over time, so has the conceptual relationship between "laws of nature" and human laws.

Our principal thesis is that Western jurisprudence, together with science, has contributed significantly to the mechanistic modern worldview; since modernity produced the materialistic orientation and extractive mentality of the Industrial Age, which lies at the root of today's global ecological, social, and economic crisis, both scientists and jurists must share some responsibility for the current state of the world. Because the critical target of this book is the dominant global system of knowledge and power, this book discusses only Western law and Western science. There is no ethnocentrism in this choice—only the urgency to place responsibility where it belongs.

At the forefront of science, a radical change of paradigms—from a mechanistic to a systemic and ecological worldview—is now emerging. The very essence of this paradigm shift is a fundamental change of metaphors: from seeing the world as a machine to understanding it as a network of ecological communities. Moreover, the science of ecology has shown us that nature sustains the web of life through a set of ecological principles that are generative rather than extractive.

A corresponding paradigm shift has yet to happen both in jurisprudence and in the public conception of the law. It is now urgently needed, since the major problems of our time are systemic problems, and our global crisis is an ecological crisis in the broadest sense of the term. In this book, we call for a profound change of legal paradigms, leading to a new ecological order in human law.

Throughout the book we discuss three interrelated themes: the relationship between science and jurisprudence, and between the "laws of nature" and human laws; the contributions of jurisprudence and science to the modern worldview, and of modernity to the current global crisis; and the recent paradigm shift in science and the need for a corresponding shift in law to develop an ecological legal order.

The book is divided into an Introduction and ten chapters. In the Introduction, we present our principal thesis. In Chapter 1, we clarify some misconceptions about the similarities and differences between science and jurisprudence.

In Chapter 2, we review the evolution of Western scientific thought from antiquity to the Scientific Revolution and the Enlightenment, culminating in a mechanistic paradigm that advocates the human domination of nature; views the material world as a machine; postulates the concept of objective, unchangeable "laws of nature"; and promotes a rationalist, atomistic view of society.

In Chapter 3, we discuss the corresponding evolution of Western legal thought, which resulted in a mechanistic legal paradigm in which social reality is viewed as an aggregate of discrete individuals and ownership as an individual right, protected by the state. Indeed, we present ownership and state sovereignty as the two organizing principles of legal modernity. Moreover, we emphasize that, in the mechanistic paradigm, law has become an "objective" framework with no room for a human interpreter.

In Chapter 4, we describe the rise and principal characteristics of legal modernity, including the profound social transformation, in little more than three hundred years, from a situation of abundant commons and scarce capital to the current one of excessive capital and dramatically weak ecological commons and community ties. We also discuss the rise and domination of economic science, the fiction of corporations as legal "persons," and the reductionist idea of a single legal order.

In Chapter 5, we review the paradigm shift in science from seeing the world as a machine to understanding it as a network, including the conceptual revolution in physics during the first three decades of the twentieth century and the subsequent emergence of systems thinking in the life sciences.

In Chapter 6, we show how the Romantic and evolutionary critiques of Cartesian rationality in legal thinking failed to overcome the mechanistic vision, which consequently has proved much more resilient in the law than in science.

In Chapter 7, we describe what we call the "mechanistic trap," a set of incentive schemes that "naturalize" the current situation. It is especially difficult to escape the mechanistic trap, because the status quo, looking natural rather than cultural, disempowers people.

In Chapter 8, we discuss three fundamental principles necessary to overcome the situation described in Chapter 7: disconnecting law from power and violence; making community sovereign; and making property generative.

In Chapter 9, we outline the legal structure of the "commons," the relational institution that should lie at the core of a legal system consistent with the ecological principles that sustain life on our planet.

In Chapter 10, we conclude with a first sketch of some basic principles of an "ecolegal" order, and we illustrate them with examples of current revolutionary struggles that try to make such a new order a reality.

In addition to being espoused by jurists and lawyers, the mechanistic worldview of modernity still holds sway among business and political leaders. In particular, they relentlessly pursue the persistent illusion of perpetual economic growth on a finite planet by promoting excessive consumption and a throwaway economy that is energy and resource intensive, generating waste and pollution and depleting the Earth's natural resources.

Both the current global economy and the legal order embedded in it are manifestly unsustainable, and a new ecolegal order—based on ecological and legal literacy, fair sharing of the commons, civic engagement, and participation—is urgently needed. However, such a new legal system cannot be imposed, nor can it be described precisely at this point. We need to allow it to emerge, and we urge all citizens to participate in this process. The assertion that each one of us can participate now in the making of the new ecolegal order is the hopeful conclusion of our book.

Leading Scholars in Science and Jurisprudence

SCIENCE　　　　　**JURISPRUDENCE**

ANTIQUITY

Aristotle (384–322 B.C.E.)

Proposed a grand synthesis of the natural philosophy of antiquity; saw the world as *kósmos*, an ordered and harmonious structure in which all parts follow an innate purpose (*télos*). Considered the material world to be composed of varying combinations of four elements—earth, water, air, and fire.

Introduced a fundamental distinction between customary and enacted law; gave a central position to private property, which he legitimized by reason.

Gaius (fl. 130–180 C.E.)

Put existing brief legal texts into a systematic order in his *Institutiones*; identified taxonomy and legal patterns still used today.

SCIENCE   **JURISPRUDENCE**

ANTIQUITY

Justinian I (483–565 C.E.)

Sponsored the revision and simplification of Roman law in the *Corpus iuris civilis* (534 C.E.). Also known as the Code of Justinian, it is considered the most important law book ever written, containing the "DNA" of global law.

MIDDLE AGES

Thomas Aquinas (1225–1274)

Created the synthesis of Aristotelian philosophy and medieval Christian theology known as scholasticism.

Bartolus of Saxoferrato (1313–1357)

Developed the *mos italicus* (the Italian way), an early systemic analysis of law that for practical reasons develops legal principles abstracted from individual conflicts about property.

RENAISSANCE

Leonardo da Vinci (1452–1519)

Created a unique synthesis of art, science, and design. An early systemic thinker, he developed a multidisciplinary science of living forms.

Francisco de Vitoria (1492–1546)

Founded the Spanish school of natural law; attempted to construct a scientific legal system for a just society under God-given natural laws.

Sir Edward Coke (1552–1634)

Last of the great medieval jurists; allied with barons and supported the common law against the monarchy.

SCIENTIFIC REVOLUTION

Galileo Galilei (1564–1642)

Focused on quantification combined with mathematics.

SCIENTIFIC REVOLUTION

Francis Bacon (1561–1626)

Passionately advocated for the empirical scientific method and the domination of nature.

Served as Lord Chancellor of England. An outstanding lawyer, he was an early champion of legal absolutism.

René Descartes (1596–1650)

Hugo Grotius (1583–1645)

Developed the mechanistic worldview. A towering figure of seventeenth-century philosophy, he was a brilliant mathematician and a very influential scientist.

Founded the northern school of natural law, which was based on a Cartesian vision of rational natural laws.

Thomas Hobbes (1588–1679)

Fully developed the absolutist theory of state sovereignty that, together with absolute ownership, is the foundation of modern legal thought.

SCIENTIFIC REVOLUTION

Isaac Newton (1642–1727)

Developed a mathematical formulation of the mechanistic worldview.
His grand synthesis of Galileo,
Bacon, and Descartes became known
as Newtonian physics.

The concept of the "laws of nature"
was firmly established because of
Newton's tremendous prestige.

ENLIGHTENMENT ("AGE OF REASON")

John Locke (1632–1704)

Jean Domat (1625–1696)

Elaborated an atomistic view of
society, described in terms of its
basic building blocks, individual
human beings; invented a "natural
right" to private property.

Determined the triumph of the
conception of rational natural laws,
based on protecting private property
against state sovereignty.

Critical reasoning, empiricism,
and individualism became dominant
values, together with a secular and
materialistic orientation.

Developed a rationalist and
atomistic vision of the French
legal system, which would be
incorporated into the Napoleonic
Code in 1804.

ENLIGHTENMENT ("AGE OF REASON")

William Blackstone (1723–1780)

Appointed as the first professor of English law; defined private property in absolute terms borrowed from rationalist natural law; emphasized the owner-centric idea of jurisprudence.

THE NINETEENTH CENTURY

Johann Wolfgang von Goethe (1749–1832)

Ardently opposed the mechanistic worldview; became central figure of the Romantic movement of poets, philosophers, and scientists.

Friedrich Karl von Savigny (1779–1861)

Strongly criticized rationalist natural law. His emphasis on legal evolution in opposition to legal absolutism had been developed earlier in the works of Montesquieu and several Scottish jurists.

THE NINETEENTH CENTURY

Charles Darwin (1809–1882)

Developed evolutionary thought—a
decisive challenge to the immutability
of the Newtonian world-machine.

THE TWENTIETH CENTURY

Werner Heisenberg (1901–1976)

Helped to found the study of
quantum physics; emphasized the
importance of the human observer in
atomic phenomena.

François Gény (1861–1959)

Criticized the mechanistic
paradigm and scientific positivism;
emphasized the creative role of the
legal interpreter.

THE ECOLOGY OF LAW

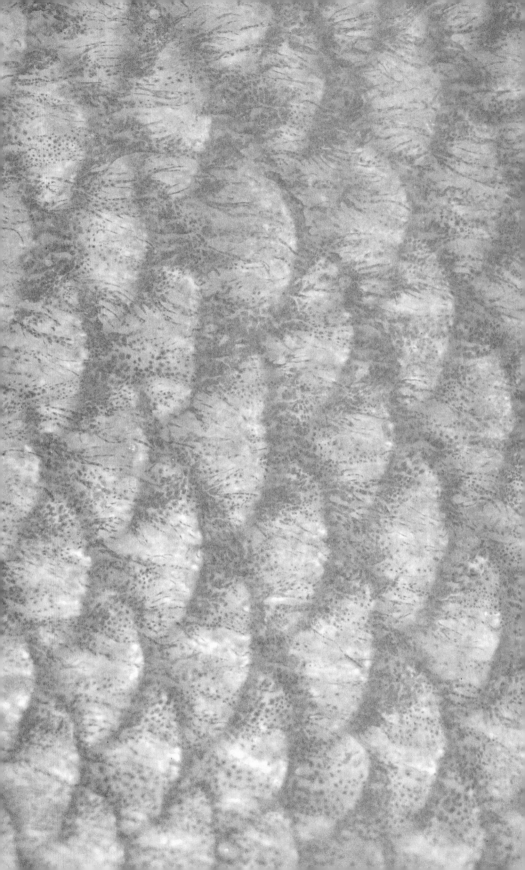

The Laws of Nature and the Nature of Law

The Nile perch is among the largest of freshwater fish, capable of achieving a length of more than 6 feet and a weight of more than 400 pounds. The perch is native to the sub-Sahara and is found not only in the Nile but also in the Congo, the Niger, and other rivers, as well as in Lake Chad and other major basins. For more than half a century, however, it also has been found in Lake Victoria in east Africa, where it is not native, and where it has subsequently become one of the best-known examples of the unintended consequences of introducing a species to an ecosystem. A brilliant documentary by Hubert Sauper, *Darwin's Nightmare*, made this story known to a wide public in 2004.

As a top-level predator of extraordinary size, might, and greed, the perch will eat most anything, including its own species. It has a potential life span of sixteen years, giving it enormous potential for ongoing destruction. Its introduction by humans to Lake Victoria for commercial harvest has caused the disappearance of most of the endemic species in the lake and has created disastrous social and economic consequences. For instance, large-scale fishing operations, typically geared toward export, have robbed many local people of their traditional livelihood in the fishing trades. Towns along the lakeshore arose to service fishery workers, but these towns offer little in the way of basic services such as water or electricity. Local people who have not been assimilated into the new local cash economy have been forced to leave their homes in search of work. Prostitution, AIDS, and drug abuse by street children are rampant. Moreover, the Nile perch cannot be sun-dried in the traditional way but instead must be preserved through smoking, which has caused a severe depletion of firewood in the region.

It is difficult to find a better metaphor for the impact of the modern economic and legal paradigm on a local community. Across the world, over and over again, this paradigm of short-term extraction, state sovereignty, and private ownership fueled by money (itself a legal abstraction concentrated in the private hands of corporate banks) has produced huge benefits to a few at the expense of the environment and local communities. State and capitalist ownership, most notably the modern transnational corporation, not unlike the Nile perch itself, displays cannibalistic tendencies, with various players eating each other by way of war or takeover.[1]

Similar examples can be found all over the world. In the Pacific Northwest, a century of extractive clear-cutting practices in forestry have devastated the landscape, silted streams, and endangered salmon habitat. As the trees have disappeared, so have many local livelihoods. In California and across the West and Southwest, the overuse of water for growing desert populations and industrial agriculture has resulted in depleted aquifers and overstressed watersheds, worsening the effects of drought and threatening livelihoods and food security. Across the world, food shortages, disease, and overpopulation, often resulting from short-term economic incentives or other human action, have played a part in creating income disparity and environmental degradation.[2]

Just as the Nile perch has devastated its new environment and may potentially eat itself out of Lake Victoria, it is no exaggeration to say that human civilization, together with many higher forms of life, may disappear from the planet unless we can reverse our extractive, destructive ways in time. Nor is it too far-fetched an idea to see modern capitalist institutions behaving as the Nile perch in many places of this world. For instance, the disruption caused by the development projects of global corporations to attract rich tourists in the global south is never taken into consideration by the celebrative narratives of the development and economic growth they produce.

But deciding on a remedy first requires understanding how this system came about. We did not end up with our current short-sighted economic and political system by accident, although, as we shall see, it wasn't quite planned, either. Our main thesis in this book, as stated in our Preface, is that jurisprudence (the theory of law), together with science, has contributed significantly to the mechanistic modern worldview. Because modernity, at least since the seventeenth century, has produced the materialistic orientation and extractive mentality of the Industrial Age, which lies at the roots of today's global crisis, both scientists and jurists must share some responsibility for the current state of the world. As we explore the relationship between science and law, we shall discover that jurisprudence is an intellectual discipline with a history and a conceptual structure that show surprising parallels to those of natural science. We shall also see that their mutual interactions evolved over time, as did the relationship between the "laws of nature" and human laws.

In science, the mechanistic paradigm that began in the six-teenth and seventeenth centuries includes an emphasis on quanti-fication, introduced by Galileo Galilei, and on the human domi-nation of nature, championed by Francis Bacon; the view of the material world as a machine, separate from the mind, advanced by René Descartes; Isaac Newton's concept of objective, unchange-able "laws of nature"; and a rationalist, atomistic view of society promoted by John Locke.

In jurisprudence, the rationalist, mechanistic paradigm, devel-oped by seventeenth-century jurists like Hugo Grotius and Jean Domat, views reality as an aggregate of discrete definable compo-nents, owners whose individual rights are protected by the state. Indeed, ownership and state sovereignty, respectively championed by John Locke and Thomas Hobbes, are the two organizing prin-ciples of legal modernity.[3] Moreover, still in the Cartesian tradi-tion, the law is seen as an "objective" framework separate from the individual subject.

During the past three decades, a radically new paradigm has emerged at the forefront of science.[4] At the heart of this change of paradigms from a mechanistic to a holistic and ecological world-view we find a profound change of metaphor: from seeing the world as a machine to understanding it as a network. Networks, of course, are patterns of relationships; hence, understanding life in terms of networks requires an ability to think in terms of relation-ships and patterns. In science, this new way of thinking is known as "systems thinking," or systemic thinking. We have also realized that nature sustains life through a set of ecological principles that are generative rather than extractive.

A corresponding paradigm shift has not yet happened either in jurisprudence or in the public understanding of law. Such a shift is now urgently needed, since the major problems of our time are systemic problems—all interconnected and interdependent—and our global crisis is an ecological crisis in the broadest sense of the term.

In this book, we call for a profound change of legal paradigms, leading to a new "ecology of law." At the heart of this new eco-logical legal order lies a view of social reality not as being an aggregate of individual "building blocks" but rather as being composed of social networks and communities. Law, in this view, is not an objective structure, but emerges from actively engaged citizen and legal communities as the legal embodiment of their self-organization.[5]

FROM HOLISM TO MECHANISM

Until the end of the Middle Ages, cultures around the world ob-served nature very closely and adapted their way of life accord-ingly. Their observations were often couched in religious or myth-ological language, and, in general, nature and its laws were seen as emanating from God or some other divine power. These beliefs implied rules for human behavior that everyone was expected to follow; even law itself was a deeply spiritual concept, based on obligation and on the proper role of an individual within a com-munity and in relation to the life-sustaining earth.[6] The Latin term *agriculture*, or "cultivation of the land," reflects this deep sense of

obligation, which was perceived as a process of creation and generation through labor, knowledge, and skill, and certainly not as a
process of extracting "value."

This early holistic, communal conception of the universe and
the planet continued to be dominant until the Scientific Revolution
of the sixteenth and seventeenth centuries, which championed the
study of matter and brought forth the mechanistic science of Galileo, Descartes, and Newton. Nature was now seen as a machine
made up of discrete, measurable parts. Galileo postulated that
scientists should restrict themselves to studying the measurable,
quantifiable properties of material bodies, such as shape, number, and movement. Other qualitative properties, such as color,
sound, taste, or smell, were merely subjective mental projections
and should be excluded from the domain of science and its goal of
describing nature in mathematical terms.

Galileo's strategy of directing scientists' attention to the quantifiable properties of matter proved extremely successful in classical physics, but also exacted a heavy toll. During the centuries
after Galileo, the focus on quantities was extended from the study
of matter to all natural and social phenomena. The subsequent
mechanistic scientific worldview of Descartes and Newton, in addition to excluding qualitative properties, also omitted more complex qualities, such as beauty, health, or ethical sensibility. The
emphasis on quantification prevented scientists for several centuries from understanding many essential properties of life.

POWER IN SCIENCE AND LAW

As the holistic view of nature was replaced by the metaphor of the
world as a machine, the goal of science became knowledge that
could be used to dominate and control nature. A similar movement was afoot in legal thought. Jurists like Grotius and Domat,
both contemporaries of Descartes, promoted the view of reality
as an aggregate of discrete definable components (free individual
actors), and ownership as an individual right, guaranteed by the
state, to develop nature, that is, to transform it into physical ob-

jects. Indeed, ownership and state sovereignty—championed in the seventeenth century by John Locke and Thomas Hobbes, respectively—are the two organizing principles of legal modernity, known to jurists also as legal absolutism.[7] At the same time, law began to be seen as an "objective" framework separated from its interpreter—another legacy of Descartes that is still present in today's legal thinking.

The human dominance of nature advocated by lawyer and scientist Francis Bacon has produced the ongoing exploitation and destruction of nature with ever more powerful technologies.[8] The world of Bacon and his contemporaries was characterized by a tremendous abundance of common resources, such as forests and fisheries, and of communal institutions, such as professional guilds and village structures, known collectively as *the commons*. The capital needed to develop manufacturing and industry was dramatically scarce. Institutions such as individual private property, stock corporations, and sovereign states—and also general freedom of contract and fault liability—were created to transform some of these commons into concentrated capital. The success of this institutional scheme has been staggering. In less than three hundred years the conditions have been reversed: today we experience a dramatic scarcity of commons and an overabundance of capital.[9]

The law has played a fundamental role in "naturalizing" this power.[10] The sovereign state and the sovereign private owner have acted as two mighty allies in the destruction of the previous legal order based on social relationship and the adaptation of humans to the ecological requirements of nature. Law has served as an instrument of human domination over nature, incrementally pushing people away from participating in nature's reproductive processes, overcoming the old medieval organic wisdom. Henceforth, nature was seen as "belonging" to humankind, and nature's main purpose was deemed the satisfaction of human needs. While the daily experience of life in traditional agricultural civilizations, hard and brutish as it might have been, linked human communities to the land and sustained a symbiotic relationship with it, law and science converged with the rise of modernity to intellectually contrast humankind with all other creatures, "freeing" humans from our ecological chains. Other creatures were seen to live in a "state of nature," but humans no longer belonged to the same category. Through science, humans could understand nature; through technology, we could transform it; and through the legal institutions of property and sovereignty, nature's essence could be transformed into a commodity, a physical object that humans could exploit or "improve."[11]

Today, the current mainstream vision is essentially the same, which is why most people considered it "natural"—legal and even beneficial to development and growth—to introduce the Nile perch to Lake Victoria. The general public broadly shares the conviction that, in relation to a common holding such as a lake or any other potentially profitable resource, the natural self-interested behavior is to benefit from it by extracting value. Introducing the Nile perch, developing an uncontaminated cove, digging Alaska for oil, and fracking the land are all exercises of economic freedom protected by private property, which grants sovereignty to individuals. The only agent that can check such freedom is the sovereign state in a zero-sum equation between the two (more state government equals less freedom of property; more freedom equals less government), itself perceived as a law of nature. If the law (an external limit) does not restrict a given action, the rational actor is assumed free to extract. Moreover, these apparently mutually exclusive domains are deemed to be governed by an irrefutable logic: more market equals less state, and more state implies less market.

MARKET AND STATE

This mechanistic vision of property and sovereignty is responsible for the dramatic state of affairs on our planet. Property rights, granting power to corporations and supported by the state, made it natural for BP to increase profits by neglecting various safety measures on its *Deepwater Horizon* oil rig, which resulted in the devastating pollution of the Gulf of Mexico; and for Exxon to avoid fixing the radar on the *Exxon Valdez*, leading to the destruction of the ecosystem of Prince William Sound in Alaska. Through this culturally constructed mechanism of free extraction, the subprime mortgage bubble was produced, AIDS and malaria have remained untreated in Africa, arms trafficking is rampant, and financial "creativity" has endangered the lives of many people. The concentration of power in state institutions determined the nuclear catastrophes of Chernobyl and Fukushima; and the view of nature as a machine, to be adapted to human use, has led to the tragedy of Lake Victoria and similar ecological catastrophes.

Modern property rights, as structured, not only determine the behavior of participants in the legal system but also, most importantly, display a remarkable independence even from the power concentrated in governments.[12] When corporations are granted charters that allow them to "live" forever but to legally avoid long-term consequences, they can easily evade their civic responsibilities. The law, built on property rights centered on the individual, has a life of its own and can defeat even the most well-intentioned and mighty forces of change.

Today, all political debates are firmly anchored in the powerful academic discipline of economics, which, by successfully claiming to be an exact science, determines policy making and legislation. Unfortunately, economics still applies a short-term, reductionist, linear, and quantitative bias typical of traditional scientific thought, a consequence of the mechanistic paradigm.[13] Having conquered the legal system through economics, this obsolete mainstream view, rooted in the duopoly of property and state, now fuels our ecologically destructive practices. So-called economic laws produce major distortions because they are based on the assumption that it is natural and desirable for an institution to set growth targets that induce extractive individual behavior while discouraging virtuous practices. For example, if one considers water as just another commodity, the laws of "scarcity" deem it desirable that water should carry a price and not be freely available for human use. Economists make much out of this observation by telling us that the increase of price reduces the amount consumed, so they use an ecological argument to recommend that public water systems be transferred to for-profit corporations. Unfortunately, the laws of "supply and demand" make it natural for a corporation to sell as much of its product as possible in order to grow and prosper. So corporations profit from the excessive lengths of showers that many Western people enjoy. Rather than taking into consideration the long-term need for ecological balance, economic actors "naturally" act to expand their own business opportunities with more investment in producing individual wants by means of advertising, so that the production of useless, environmentally harmful commodities is their top priority.[14] Shampoo companies, for example, promote the desire for long, refreshing showers as a condition of individual self-fulfillment, and mineral water companies induce the need to drink bottled water transported in polluting trucks because it is as much as five hundred times more profitable than tap water. In California, for example, the average cost of tap water is $1.60 per one thousand gallons while the average cost of bottled water is about 560 times higher at 90 cents per one gallon.[15]

The disastrous effects of our laws and economy are rather clear at this point, but this understanding has not affected policy making. Instead, the legal system has cast our unsustainable model of development in stone as property rights. Current political and economic debates are dominated by fragmentation and linear thinking, with an especially unwarranted faith in both technological progress and infinite growth on a finite planet. The idea of "development" is fundamentally quantitative; it is rooted in seventeenth-century notions of "improvement" and today employs the concept of gross domestic product as the measure of social wealth. But development does not recognize that unrestrained extraction and exploitation of natural and human resources is at odds with the fundamental principles of ecology. The violation of these principles has consequences as lethal as ignoring the law of gravity while climbing a mountain, but because the effects are spread across time and often are not located in any specific individual, they are more difficult to vividly depict in the immediate terms that might spur action. Skepticism, very often itself corporate-determined, can thus be alive and well even in the face of such scientific truths as human-induced global warming.[16]

Both the state and the market are determined by human-made law but are presented as natural realities that can be described with scientific rigor as objects of an external world. However, as we will see, rather than being natural, the state and the market are only cultural products. We often lose sight of the fact that they do not represent an immutable status quo but can be, and actually are, changed all the time by human agency. This mutable characteristic of law, if properly harnessed, represents a path away from destruction and toward a generative, ecologically sustainable human endeavor. To take this path, we first need to carefully reassess the current worldviews of science and law.

A NEW SCIENTIFIC PERCEPTION

Over the last three decades, the forefront of science has seen a dramatic change of paradigms from the mechanistic and reductionist worldview of Descartes and Newton to a systemic and ecological worldview. We have discovered that the material world, ultimately, is a network of inseparable patterns of relationships; that the planet as a whole is a living, self-regulating system. The view of the human body as a machine and of the mind as a separate entity is being replaced by one that sees not only the brain but also the immune system, the bodily tissues, and even each cell as a living, cognitive system. Evolution is no longer seen as a competitive struggle for existence, but is rather viewed as a cooperative dance in which creativity and the constant emergence of novelty are the driving forces. With the new emphasis on complexity, networks, and patterns of organization, a new science of qualities is slowly emerging.

At the very heart of this change of paradigms from a mechanistic to a systemic view of life we find a fundamental change of metaphors: from seeing the world as a machine to understanding it as a network. As we have mentioned, a corresponding paradigm shift has not happened in law or in economics. In this book, we plead for a change of the legal paradigm, inspired by the recognition of basic principles of ecology and by the new systemic thinking in contemporary science.

The mechanistic scientific approach has served us, and continues to serve us, very well in many ways—one can still build a bridge using the principles of Newtonian physics, for example. But the limitations of this approach are becoming increasingly clear, particularly in relation to law. By protecting corporate property rights of extraction as natural, we have created a kind of Frankenstein's monster in which individual actors, who are actually the creators of law, no longer seem to have the power to curb the more destructive results that this approach encourages.

Despite the systemic thinking at the forefront of science, the disciplines of law and economics continue to support a short-term vision, viewing reality in a mechanistic way. They put at the center of their vision an atomized and abstract individual owner. This atom can exercise his ownership of the Earth by extracting value from the commons at the expense of others, thus generating the famous metaphor known as the tragedy of the commons, which is a classic example of self-fulfilling prophecy.[17] The dominant concept of ownership as an individual right, protected by the state to allow short-term accumulation and extraction, became the natural building block of the current legal order; as such it has been responsible for crisis after crisis. The current collective perception of law as an "objective" or preexisting framework through which the behavior of the individual atoms can be classified as legal or illegal, far from being "natural," is just a cultural construction of modernity. Modern law thus embodies the Cartesian separation of an objectified legal order—analogous to Descartes's *res extensa* (the object of thought)—that is essentially separate from the everyday realm of human agency located in the domain of the *res cogitans* (the thinking subject) (see chapter 2).[18]

This state of affairs is not inevitable. Humans were able to employ science and law to transform common holdings into a commodity and then into capital; we also have the ability to reverse this path, transforming some of our now overabundant capital into renewed commons. An ecologically transformed law can transform capital into natural commons by producing a sustained investment into a sharing economy, into ecologically compatible architecture, or into environmental care. Such law could also transform capital into social and cultural commons by protecting the Internet against privatization or by mandating the deployment of systems of generative property law instead of protecting the freedom of extraction.

This process is urgently needed and overdue. It is as simple and revolutionary as the Copernican revolution, which at the dawn of modernity displaced the Earth from the center of the solar system in favor of the Sun as a result of new knowledge. This process requires that we now, as a consequence of our new ecological knowledge, displace the individual owner from the center of the legal system in favor of the commons. To do this we must rethink the most intimate structure of the law to reflect the basic principles of ecology and the new systemic thinking of contemporary science: no mechanistic separation between subject and object; no individual atom, but community and relationship as building blocks of the legal order. The reality follows what we collectively think and do.

The legal order is the most important vehicle through which a worldview is enforced and transformed into social action, and thus human law is also the agency through which we may implement new ideas and values. We must rethink our human laws and their relationship with the laws governing the ecology of a living planet. Such a rethinking, a kind of Copernican revolution in the law, must use nature as a mentor and model, putting the commons and a long-term vision at center stage. We must move from thinking of a "mechanism of law" and move toward an "ecology of law." We shall discuss the nature of such a paradigm shift in law, and compare it to the change of worldview that is now happening in science, in detail in the following chapters. As a kind of preview, the basic points of our argument are summarized in the table on page 13.

SCIENCE	LAW

The Mechanistic Paradigm ("World as Machine")

Physical reality is an aggregate of separate building blocks.	Social reality is an aggregate of discrete individuals.
Scientific knowledge is used to dominate and control nature.	Law is used to protect extractive ownership as an individual right.
Scientific truth (the "laws of nature") can be arrived at through reasoning.	Natural law is based on human reason.
Scientific descriptions are objective, independent of the human observer.	Law is an objective framework separate from a human interpreter.

The Systemic, Ecological Paradigm ("World as Network")

Physical reality is a network of inseparable relationships.	Social reality is composed of social networks and communities.
Scientific knowledge ("ecological literacy") is to be used to learn from and cooperate with nature.	The new ecological legal order is to be used by ecoliterate citizens to protect and generate commons.
Scientific knowledge is always approximate; it emerges from a process of establishing consensus in the scientific community.	Law emerges from actively engaged citizens in self-organizing communities.
Scientific descriptions depend on the human observer and on the process of acquiring knowledge.	Law is what is deemed to be law by civic and legal communities; it depends on human interpretations of social reality.

THE ECOLOGY OF LAW

In the strict scientific sense, ecology is the science of relationships between the members of an ecological community and their environment. In this sense, then, the ecology of law refers to a legal order that is consistent with and honors the basic principles of ecology. The ecology of law implies a process of transforming legal institutions from being machines of extraction, rooted in the mechanistic functioning of private property and state authority, into institutions based on ecological communities. The ecology of law seeks a quality of economic life aimed at nurturing and preserving nature in the interest of future generations and overall human survival. The law should mimic the natural strategies of long-term ecological survival, including the reduction of waste and consumption.

In a broader, more metaphorical sense, ecology refers to a pattern of relationships that define the context for a certain phenomenon.[19] For example, the ecology of education would refer to the relationships between education and knowledge, careers, economics, wisdom, ethics, politics, and so on, all of which would be perceived as being part of a total pattern of relationships. In this broad sense, we use the term "the ecology of law" to refer to a legal order that does not see the law as a separate social field independent from politics, economics, justice, religion, social norms of good behavior, morality, and so forth. Nor does this conception separate the law into a domain of facts—how the law *is*—and a domain of values—how the law *ought to be*.

In other words, an ecological vision of law does not reduce law to a professionalized, preexisting, objective framework "out there," separate from the behavior it regulates and tries to determine. Instead, law is always a process of *"commoning,"* a long-term collective action in which communities, sharing a common purpose and culture, institutionalize their collective will to maintain order and stability in the pursuit of social reproduction. Thus the commons—an open network of relationships—rather than the individual, is the building block of the ecology of law and what we call an "ecolegal" order. Such an ecolegal order is built on the recognition that human survival on this planet is not guaranteed by the destruction of life and by the domination of nature in search of growth. Rather, it seeks a quality of economic life aimed at nurturing our living planet and focusing on generative, complex patterns of relationships.

In order to work properly, such a legal order will require a basic public understanding of its operation and nature, because the law is deeply affected and determined by its component parts, the social actors—individuals. Today, such basic understanding and awareness of the law is dramatically lacking. The revolution we need, like those that led us here (Copernican, scientific, industrial, bourgeois), is a collective enterprise. It is independent of race, class, or gender but requires everyone to develop some basic ecological literacy as well as an understanding of the nature and function of law in today's world. We must learn from our history, looking at both law and science as cultural artifacts, collective enterprises, parts of the fascinating and dramatic journey of humanity.

CHAPTER 1

Science and Law

In our broad sweep through Western intellectual history, we shall encounter many great scientists and great jurists—on some occasions even embodied in the same person—whose ideas shaped the coevolution of the concepts of the laws of nature and of human laws. To tell this story clearly we first need to unravel some common misconceptions about the similarities and differences between science and jurisprudence.

Both science and law include a theoretical and an applied component. Applied science produces, among other things, technology—the development of specific technical capabilities. Thus science and technology operate in two strongly connected but quite separate domains, and actually technology often takes on a life of its own.

A similar phenomenon occurs in law. A clear distinction exists between legal theory and legal practice.[1] On the one hand, legal theory (also known as jurisprudence, or the philosophy of law) is a theoretical inquiry into legal phenomena. Human laws are the subject matter of jurisprudence just as the laws of nature are the subject matter of science. Legal practice, on the other hand, corresponds to technology in many ways. Like technology, it has a life quite autonomous from legal science, and lawyers sometimes distinguish between "law in books" and "law in action."[2]

JUS AND *LEX*

In order to better understand these parallels, we need to introduce a fundamental distinction that is quite obvious to lawyers but not to the general public. In English, the single term "law" is used to describe two distinct phenomena that many languages other than English use two different terms to describe. Latin jurists, at the dawn of the Western legal tradition, distinguished the idea of *jus* from that of *lex*. Similar juxtapositions can be found in many languages—*droit* and *loi* in French, *derecho* and *ley* in Spanish, *diritto* and *legge* in Italian, *Recht* and *Gesetz* in German, *pravo* and *zakon* in Russian, and so on.

In all these languages, the meaning of law as *jus* indicates the law as a conceptual framework that abstracts from the reality of human relationships a set of more-or-less coherent principles and rules that are general enough to be reproduced in a variety of settings. This framework is theoretically discussed, elaborated, and continually modified by lawyers serving in a variety of professional capacities (such as professors, judges, practitioners, and legal philosophers). The work of these jurists continually adapts the framework of the law to changing social, political, and cultural conditions, thus "making the law" in these different professional capacities. The roles of academic scholars, who engage in theoretical work and teach the law as a university discipline, and of judges, who in their judicial capacity coherently apply these principles and rules to solve actual social conflicts, are particularly significant in the Western legal tradition.[3]

Jurisprudence, the theoretical discipline of the law, is acknowledged by lawyers, but not by the general public, who often do not appreciate the richness of this intellectual component in the laws that regulate their lives. People usually reduce the idea of law to what is meant by the term *lex* (plural *leges*; the Latin root of "legal" and "legislation"): a concrete rule that governs a factual situation and reflects the will of a governing authority endowed with the power to enforce it. Such specific laws are usually harmonized within the grand scheme of legal theory by the interpretive activity of legal professionals (again in their various institutional capacities) and thus become part of law as a *legal system* (i.e., the orderly combination of particular laws into a whole, according to rational principles). Thus, the legal systems of the United States or France are not mere aggregates of enacted rules in those countries. The laws governing us in each territory include the highly intellectual dimension of *jus*, which is a deep part of our culture.[4]

An objective legal order determines and defines subjective individual rights, such as property rights or personal rights. In the languages mentioned above, the words corresponding to *jus* translate as the English word "right," a term that evokes both the idea of an objective legal framework *and* the idea of a subjective right. In Western jurisprudence, rights are seen as zones of protected freedom.[5]

The meaning of law as *lex* is value-neutral; it refers to the institutional force that produces and formally enacts it, thus making it binding. The broader meaning of law as *jus*, in contrast, is laden with desirable values, being associated with the ideas of just, straight, and right (as opposed to wrong).

DESCRIPTIVE VERSUS NORMATIVE LAWS

A key difference between the laws of nature and human laws seems to be that the former are *descriptive* (giving information about something in the natural world) while the latter are *normative* (prescribing a standard of behavior for humans). However, as we explore the surprising parallels between how these laws have been conceptualized in science and in jurisprudence, we shall see that this clear-cut distinction must also be modified. On the one hand, a descriptive element occurs in the practice of jurists abstracting the relevant laws from a specific network of social relationships. On the other hand, recent discoveries in science, especially in ecology and climate science, suggest strongly that the ecological principles evolved by ecosystems over billions of years to sustain the web of life must be understood as normative laws for human conduct if we are to overcome our global environmental crisis.

"NATURAL LAW" AND THE "LAWS OF NATURE"

In our comparisons of the laws of nature and human laws we will
have to be careful to avoid confusion between the terms *natural
law* and *laws of nature*.[6] In legal parlance, a "natural law" is one that
should be binding only if it is consistent with some higher validating principle, which might stem from a divine source or from human reason. This understanding is in direct contrast to a school of
thought called *legal positivism*. According to legal positivists, law
derives its binding power from a sovereign authority, regardless of
whether that law is just, fair, or even rational.

The origin of the term "laws of nature" itself is rather fascinating. Throughout the earlier centuries of Western science, various
terms were used for the short, concise statements or equations in
which scientists like to summarize their theories. They were called
propositions, rules, axioms, principles, maxims, and so on. During the second half of the seventeenth century, the expression
"laws of nature," which had rarely been used before, came into
frequent use, and in subsequent centuries it completely replaced
the previously used terms.

The concept of "laws of nature" was often used explicitly in
analogy with human laws. As human laws were binding rules of
conduct for a community, so the laws of nature were understood
as an order legislated for the entire universe by a divine authority.
This analogy caused several philosophical and theological problems. Human laws, notoriously prone to inconsistency, variation,
and violation, seemed a poor model for the allegedly immutable
regularity of the natural order. Moreover, it was difficult to understand how inanimate matter could be said to "obey" laws in any
but a metaphorical sense. In spite of these philosophical difficulties, the concept of the laws of nature became an integral part of
natural philosophy or natural science. How this came to be is an
interesting story, to which we shall return in Chapter 2.

In the twentieth century, when scientists became increasingly
aware of the approximate nature of all their models and theories,

they seem to have stopped referring to the regularities they discovered as laws, except for references to the well-known "laws" formulated in previous centuries.

LAWYERS AND SCIENTISTS

Lawyers and scientists are often seen as very different kinds of people. It is usually said that students who do poorly in math and science are those who sign up for law school. Despite many exceptions, especially in American law schools where legal training is offered to students as a graduate program, this conviction is difficult to dispel. Yet because of the difficulties of a career in science, bright young people, after spending a few years in scientific research, often settle for law school, which promises them a more secure and lucrative future. Even these students tend to interpret law school as a second life, a complete shift to a domain of activity unrelated to their previous one. The only exceptions, perhaps, are patent lawyers, who must add some understanding of science to their legal knowledge in order to argue for the innovative nature of the invention they seek to patent.

This segregation is confirmed by the common stereotypes of these two disciplines and their representatives. While scientists are perceived as absentminded, casually dressed individuals who live in a refined world of abstract theory with little practical reality, lawyers are usually perceived as formally dressed people who are practically oriented, concentrating mainly on trivialities (such as negotiating their retaining fee) and engaging professionally in all sorts of nitty-gritty social intercourse—the kind of things that normal people, although worried by them, would rather not have to deal with themselves.

A few years ago, a very distinguished and highly theoretically minded Harvard law professor was appointed for a semester as a visiting fellow at a center for advanced interdisciplinary studies at another Ivy League institution. All the other fellows—physicists, sociologists, anthropologists, historians, and philosophers—were engaging in highly intellectual exchanges with one another, but whenever he entered the faculty common room these conversations would stop. The professor of jurisprudence would then be approached by a sociologist asking him about how to divide the expenses of replacing the elevator in her condominium building, or by a physicist inquiring about whether his insurance company should refund him for damages produced by his current house sitters, and so on. These recurring incidents were frustrating for the professor of jurisprudence, since they undermined his self-esteem as a high-profile intellectual.

This more-or-less constructed social segregation between lawyers and scientists has not always existed, and it does not mean that the legal profession is not considered socially prestigious in many countries. Together with medicine and theology, law schools (known in Continental Europe as faculties of jurisprudence) were historically among the very first higher academic institutions in the medieval West.[7] Lawyers were among the most prestigious intellectuals throughout medieval times and certainly were not looked down upon as "ambulance chasers" by other intellectual elites, as happens in the United States today. An even cursory look into the biographies of some of the most outstanding intellectuals in the history of Western science shows some interesting surprises.

Sir Francis Bacon, one of the inventors of the modern scientific method of inquiry, was also a very outstanding lawyer. He served as lord chancellor of England—perhaps the highest, oldest, and most distinguished judicial post in Great Britain—and his struggle with Sir Edward Coke in the early seventeenth century shaped much of the current structure of Anglo-American law.[8] Sir Isaac Newton, the most popular icon of modern science before Albert Einstein, while never active as a practicing lawyer, nevertheless occupied a high legal post, that of chancellor of the exchequer. In that capacity, he chaired one of the most ancient judicial institutions of the common-law tradition, devoted to tax law issues. Newton's contemporary Gottfried Wilhelm Leibniz (1646–1716), the outstanding German philosopher and mathematician who invented differential calculus independently of Newton, also thought deeply about the practical affairs of state; he wrote voluminously on law, ethics, and politics. In the following chapters, when we sketch the parallel history of science and law in the West, several such fascinating convergences will emerge.

THE SCIENTIFIC METHOD

One of our principal tasks is the exploration of the conceptual and historical relationships between natural science and jurisprdence; thus it is important to clearly understand the nature of science before we begin. Today's modern word "science" is derived from the Latin *scientia*, which means "knowledge" in general, a meaning that was retained throughout the Middle Ages, the Renaissance, and the Scientific Revolution. What we call "science" today was known as "natural philosophy" up until the nineteenth century.

The modern understanding of science, which evolved during the eighteenth and nineteenth centuries, is that of an organized body of knowledge acquired through a particular method known as the scientific method. The characteristics of the scientific method were fully recognized only during the twentieth century and are still frequently misunderstood, especially by the general public and by lawyers.

The scientific method represents a particular way of gaining knowledge about natural and social phenomena that occurs in several stages. First, the phenomena being studied are systematically observed, and the observations are recorded as evidence, or scientific data. In some sciences, such as physics, chemistry, and biology, the systematic observation includes controlled experiments; in others, such as astronomy or paleontology, such experiments are not possible.

Next, scientists attempt to connect the data in a coherent way, free of internal contradictions. The resulting representation is known as a scientific model. Whenever possible, scientists try to formulate their models in mathematical language because of the precision and internal consistency inherent in mathematics. In many cases, however, especially in the social sciences, such attempts have been problematic because they tend to confine the scientific models to such a narrow range that they lose much of their usefulness. Thus we have come to realize over the last few decades that neither mathematical formulations nor quantitative results are essential components of the scientific method.

Finally, the theoretical model is tested by further observations and, if possible, additional experiments. If the model is found to be consistent with the results of these tests, and especially if it is capable of predicting the results of new experiments, it eventually becomes accepted as a scientific theory. The process of subjecting scientific ideas and models to repeated tests is a collective enterprise of the community of scientists, and the acceptance of the model as a theory is done by tacit or explicit consensus in that community.[9]

In practice, these stages are not neatly separated and do not always occur in the same order. For example, a scientist may formulate a preliminary generalization or hypothesis based on intuition or initial empirical data. When subsequent observations contradict the hypothesis, he or she may try to modify the hypothesis without giving it up completely. But if the empirical evidence continues to contradict the hypothesis or the scientific model, the scientist is forced to discard it in favor of a new hypothesis or model, which is then subjected to further tests. Even an accepted theory may eventually be overthrown when contradictory evidence comes to light. This method of basing all models and theories firmly on empirical evidence is the very essence of the scientific approach.

Crucial to the contemporary understanding of science is the realization that all scientific models and theories are limited and approximate. Twentieth-century science has shown repeatedly that all natural phenomena are ultimately interconnected and that their essential properties, in fact, derive from their relationships to other things. Hence, in order to explain any one phenomenon completely, we would have to understand all the others, which is obviously impossible. No matter how many connections we take into account in our scientific description of a phenomenon, we will always be forced to leave others out. Therefore, scientists can never deal with "truth" in the sense of a precise correspondence between a description and the described phenomenon. In science, we always deal with limited and approximate descriptions of reality.

To repeat, the approximate nature of scientific knowledge is a consequence of the fundamental interconnectedness of natural phenomena. In their attempts to perceive and define regularities and order in this interconnected web of relationships, scientists identify certain stable patterns as "objects," "structures," "processes," and so on. The way these identifications are made is subjective to some extent; it depends on the interpretation of the observed patterns by a particular observer. This process has forced scientists to abandon the Cartesian notion of objective scientific descriptions, independent of the observer. In contemporary science, we have to accept the fact that a subjective dimension is implicit in every scientific model or theory. This does not mean that we have to give up scientific rigor. When we speak of an "objective" description in science, we mean first and foremost a body of knowledge that is shaped, constrained, and regulated by the collective scientific enterprise, rather than being merely a collection of individual accounts. Such intersubjective validation—agreement among separate individuals—is standard practice in science and need not be abandoned.

THE LEGAL METHOD

Since interconnectedness is a fundamental feature of human existence, approximation is a central feature of legal thought as well. Jurisprudence, however, has no single "method." In different countries, in different periods of history, and sometimes even at the same time, different methods have competed with each other to grapple with the inherent complexity and variation of social life.[10] Nevertheless, the work of legal theorists shares some important characteristics with the scientific method.

The systematic observation of the facts of life, usually in the form of social conflicts between individuals or institutions, is the typical activity of the jurist. She proposes theoretical models and theories in order to group apparently very different facts within the same conceptual framework. For example, all social conflicts arising from a previous voluntary social exchange are grouped under the law of contracts; all social conflicts arising outside of any previously planned relationship are grouped under the law of torts. She tests her model with empirical evidence (that is, by consulting all the previously available records of similar social intercourses) and she accepts the limited and approximate nature of her models and theories, especially since different jurisdictions usually follow different organizational principles.

The jurist carries on her interpretation either by deduction or by induction (most often with a mix of the two), depending on whether her point of departure is a general principle, a text to be applied to specific facts, or a previous court decision to be applied by analogy. (The Anglo-American legal tradition mostly deploys an inductive method, while the Continental tradition favors the deductive one.[11]) This process has long been described as mechanical, and jurists, in order to bolster the legitimacy of their work, have usually denied any creative role in carrying it out.

As a consequence of this self-portrayal, the legal method appears in today's common perception as merely an effort of textual interpretation, an activity much different from that carried out by the scientist. While the laws of nature are hidden patterns and regularities that the scientist may discover in the course of research, human laws are considered to be mostly textual, normative words, written down in legal documents endowed with the stamp of officialdom and therefore binding and enforceable. However, our previous cursory discussion of the different meanings of human laws has already shown that reality is much more nuanced and complex.

Even written human laws are not self-evident. Their interpretation as laws is the result of a rather complex intellectual process in which the professional jurist plays a crucial role as a "maker" of the legal order. To begin with, the jurist must situate any given factual situation in a certain context, sorting the generally reproducible aspects of any social intercourse into those that are relevant and those that are not. For example, whether the driver of a car that caused an accident was black or white is deemed irrelevant in the American law of torts, while it is relevant whether the driver was driving under the influence of alcohol or not.

The lawyer will also have to locate the legal authority that will guide her analysis. Such authority may be a specific text or a precedent from case law, but not necessarily; in the current global setting, because complex transactions involve the law of more than one country, other authorities are being invoked more frequently. In fact, the interpreter can pick a given custom that she deems relevant in the specific context in which the intercourse happened, or a general principle contained in some broad constitutional language (for example, fairness, equity, or good faith).

Especially in cases where more than one sovereign state is involved, as is true for all transactions of global scope, there simply might not be a written source to consult, and the jurist will have thus to "discover" the governing law by a process of creative interpretation of the factual reality.[12] Once the given authority (textual or not) has been located, the lawyer proceeds either by deduction from the authority to the rule that applies in a given factual situation, or by induction from an aggregate of solutions of specific cases to create a general principle. In short, the legal interpreter, just like the scientist, enjoys considerable discretion in the choice of her methodological preferences. In practice, she would move back and forth between deduction and induction until she reaches a satisfactory solution.

This process happens as a concrete effort to solve a given case (if the interpreter is a judge), or to argue for a given solution of such a case (if the interpreter is an attorney); it can also be a theoretical effort to suggest the best possible principles or solutions for hypothetical cases (if the interpreter is an academic scholar). For example, in deciding whether the law accepts gay marriages, the lawyer has significant discretion in deciding whether to start from an abstract principle of equality or from a more traditional idea of the reproductive function of marriage. In all these cases, the role of the interpreter is in practice very creative. Despite long periods of denial of the interpreter's creative role, today practically every lawyer acknowledges, along with Benjamin Cardozo (1870–1938)—the U.S. Supreme Court Justice who produced quite a scandal with his "choice for candor"—that whoever interprets law, *makes* it.[13] In other words, jurists now recognize that human laws are not "out there," separate from their interpreters, and that the process of their emergence (of becoming relevant) is probably no less complex than the discovery of a "law of nature."

A CALL FOR ECOLEGAL LITERACY

The first step in creating a new ecolegal order founded on systems thinking rather than on an outdated mechanistic way of thinking is to become aware of our own power to influence law through our aggregate action. This ecological vision of the law, as we suggest for the first time in this book, can have a tremendously empowering effect. It can unleash the "power of the people," reclaiming law as a common, to create a new ecolegal order that, following our systemic understanding of the world, can protect it for future generations.

One of the great challenges of our time is to build and nurture sustainable communities—social, cultural, and physical environments in which we can satisfy our needs and aspirations without diminishing the chances of future generations. In pursuit of this goal, we must recognize that scientific positivism and reductionist economic thought, rather than being the *reality* that our laws assume and reflect, are actually ideologies serving short-term accumulative interests.[14] We can counteract these ideologies and support an eco-centric vision by using these same human laws. We need a fundamental change of perspective from economic efficiency to ecological sustainability, from private property rights to accessible commons.

A sustainable community is designed in such a way that its ways of life, businesses, economy, physical structures, and technologies do not interfere with nature's inherent ability to sustain life. The groundwork for this idea began with the 1972 publication of a radical report on a computer simulation, *The Limits to Growth*, which was authored by an MIT group led by Dennis and Donella Meadows. Following that, Lester Brown introduced the concept of sustainability in the early 1980s. A few years later, a report by the World Commission on Environment and Development, known as the Brundtland Report of 1987, presented the notion of "sustainable development."[15] The concept of sustainability has often been distorted, co-opted, and even trivialized by being used without the ecological context that gives it its proper meaning. What is sustained in a sustainable community is not economic growth, competitive advantage, or any other measure used by economists, but the entire web of life on which our long-term survival depends. The first step toward a sustainable community, naturally, must be to understand how nature sustains life. This involves a new ecological understanding of life, or "ecoliteracy," as well as a new kind of "systemic" thinking—thinking in terms of relationships, patterns, and context.

Once we have achieved some degree of ecoliteracy, we must make urgently needed shifts in law and economics. Human laws, like the laws of nature, need to be understood as manifestations of a relational order in which the individual is not alone but is connected to and shares power with other living inhabitants of the planet, who are entitled to equal access to the global commons. These inhabitants are not only other human beings but also other animals, plants, and in general all the Earth's ecosystems. The introduction of a rapacious species into a new ecosystem, for instance, would require an ecolegal review to consider the broader impacts of such an action beyond the immediate profit motive. If such an ecolegal order were present, the Nile perch would most likely not exist today in Lake Victoria; or, most important, global corporations would not be able to claim and obtain rights as though they were living creatures.

To be sustainable, human laws should serve, rather than exploit and plunder, the web of life. In law as in science, we must begin to focus on a relevant understanding of the whole rather than only the component parts. To achieve this goal, not only the laws of nature but also the nature of law should be understood by the general public. To facilitate this understanding, we shall now follow the coevolution of scientific and legal thought from antiquity to the modern era.

CHAPTER 2

From Kósmos *to Machine*

The Evolution of Early Western Scientific Thought

The historical and conceptual links between science and juris-prudence begin in Greek antiquity. From the beginning of Greek philosophy in the sixth century B.C.E., philosophers viewed the world as a *kósmos*, an ordered and harmonious structure, more a living organism rather than a mechanical system. All of nature's parts had an innate purpose and contributed to the harmonious functioning of the whole, and objects moved naturally toward their proper places in the universe. Such an explanation of natural phenomena in terms of their goals or purposes is known as *teleology*, from the Greek *télos* (purpose), and this explanation permeated virtually all of Greek philosophy and science.

The view of the cosmos as an organism implies that its general properties are reflected in each of its parts. This analogy between macrocosm and microcosm, and in particular between the Earth and the human body, was articulated most eloquently by Plato (ca. 428–348 B.C.E.) in his *Timaeus*, but it can also be found in the teachings of the Pythagoreans and other, earlier schools. Over time, this idea acquired the authority of common knowledge, which continued throughout the Middle Ages and into the Renaissance.

In early Greek philosophy, the ultimate moving force and source of all life was identified with the soul, and its principal metaphor was that of the breath of life. Indeed, the root meaning of both the Greek word for "soul," *psyché*, and the Latin word, *anima*, is "breath." Closely associated with that moving force, the breath of life that leaves the body at death, was the idea of knowing. For the early Greek philosophers, the fundamental analogy between micro- and macrocosm meant that the soul was both the source of movement and life and also that which perceives and knows. The individual soul was thought to be part of the force that moves the entire universe; accordingly, the knowledge of an individual was seen as part of a universal process of knowing. Plato called it the *anima mundi*, the "world soul."

As far as the composition of matter was concerned, Empedocles (ca. 490–430 B.C.E.) claimed that the material world was composed of varying combinations of four elements—earth, water, air, and fire. When left to themselves, these elements would settle into concentric spheres, with the Earth at the center, surrounded successively by the spheres of water, air, and fire (or light). Farther outside were the spheres of the planets, and beyond them was the sphere of the stars.

Half a century after Empedocles, an alternative theory of matter was proposed by Democritus (ca. 460–ca. 370 B.C.E.), who taught that all material objects were composed of atoms of numerous shapes and sizes, and that all observable qualities derived from the particular combinations of atoms inside the objects. His theory was so antithetical to the traditional teleological views of matter that it was pushed into the background, where it remained throughout the Middle Ages and the Renaissance. It would only surface again in the late seventeenth century, with the rise of Newtonian physics.

Even if the properties of material objects could be seen as arising from various combinations of the basic qualities inherent in the four elements, the Greek philosophers still faced the problem of how these combinations of elements acquired the specific forms we see in nature. The first philosopher to address the problem of form was Pythagoras (ca. 580–ca. 500 B.C.E.), who before the time of Plato founded a cultlike school of mathematics, organized as a commune that banned private property. Pythagoras and his disciples, the Pythagoreans, believed that numerical patterns and ratios were the origin of all forms. This association between the concrete world of natural forms and the abstract realm of numerical relationships began the link between science and mathematics that would become the foundation of classical physics in the seventeenth century.

The Pythagoreans divided the universe into two realms: the heavens, in which the stars revolve in celestial spheres according to perfect, unchanging mathematical laws; and the Earth, in which phenomena are complex, always changing, and imperfect. The distinction between the perfect, unchanging motions of the heavenly realm and the imperfect, ever-changing phenomena of the terrestrial realm meant that order decreases as one moves from the higher to the lower realms. Philosophers in subsequent centuries would point out, for example, that the regular motion of the heavenly bodies causes the regular (but slightly unpredictable) succession of the seasons; the seasons bring about the (more unpredictable) weather; and the weather influences the (very unpredictable) growth of crops.

It is not surprising, therefore, that the first precise "laws" mentioned in science were Johannes Kepler's laws of planetary motion, at the beginning of the seventeenth century. Until Galileo developed his method of concentrating on the quantifiable properties of matter that could be interlinked in terms of precise mathematical relationships, most natural philosophers were hesitant to look for precise laws in messy terrestrial phenomena.

ARISTOTLE'S SYNTHESIS OF SCIENCE

For science in subsequent centuries, the most important Greek philosopher was Aristotle (384–322 B.C.E.), the first to write systematic, professorial treatises about the main branches of learning of his time—biology, physics, metaphysics, ethics, and politics. To integrate these disciplines into a coherent theoretical framework, Aristotle created a formal system of logic and a set of unifying principles. He stated explicitly that the goal of his logic was to learn the art of scientific investigation and reasoning, which would serve as the rational instrument for all scientific work. Aristotle's synthesis and organization remained the foundation of Western science for two thousand years.

Aristotle adopted the Pythagorean antithesis between the terrestrial and the heavenly worlds. From the Earth to the sphere of the moon, he taught, all things constantly change, generating new forms and then decaying again. Above the moon, the crystalline spheres of the planets and stars revolve in eternal, unchanging motions. He also subscribed to the Platonic idea that the perfection of the celestial realm implies that the planets and stars move in perfect circles.

Aristotle taught that all spontaneously occurring activities were natural, guided by the goals inherent in physical phenomena, and hence observation was the proper means of investigating them. Experiments that altered natural conditions in order to bring to light some hidden properties of matter were unnatural, and, as such, they could not be expected to reveal the essence of the phenomena. Experiments were not a proper means of investigation, and the experimental method was not essential to Greek science.

SCHOLASTIC PHILOSOPHY

Aristotle's treatises eventually became the foundation of philosophical and scientific thought in the Middle Ages and the Renaissance. Unlike their Arab counterparts who also studied Aristotle, however, Christian medieval philosophers did not use Aristotle's texts as a basis for their own independent research. Instead, these thinkers evaluated the texts from the perspective of Christian theology. Indeed, most of them were theologians, and their practice of combining philosophy—including natural philosophy, or science—with theology became known as scholasticism.

The leading figure in this movement to weave the philosophy of Aristotle into Christian teachings was Thomas Aquinas (1225–1274). Aquinas taught that there could be no conflict between Christian faith and Aristotelian reason because the two books on which they were based—the Bible and the "book of nature"—were both authored by God. Aquinas produced a vast body of precise, detailed, and systematic philosophical writings, in which he integrated Aristotle's encyclopedic works and medieval Christian theology into a seamless whole.

The dark side of this fusion of science and theology was that any contradiction by future scientists would necessarily have to be seen as heresy. In this way, Aquinas enshrined in his writings the potential for conflicts between science and religion, which reached a dramatic climax with the burning of Giordano Bruno (1548–1600) and the trial of Galileo and have continued to the present day.

Even so, the view of nature as a book, written by God and equivalent to the Bible, opened the door for scientists to conceive of the regularities they observed in nature—for example, in the motions of the planets—as divine laws. Interestingly, however, the scholastic philosophers themselves did not use terms such as "divine laws." They were much more interested in human conduct than in natural phenomena and used the term "natural law" (*lex naturalis*) to denote the principles of correct action that were imprinted by God in the human soul.

THE SCIENTIFIC THOUGHT OF LEONARDO DA VINCI

In Western intellectual history, the Renaissance—a period stretching roughly from the beginning of the fifteenth to the end of the sixteenth century—marks the period of transition from the Middle Ages to the modern world. This period was characterized by intense exploration—both of ancient ideas and of new geographic regions of the Earth. The intellectual climate of the Renaissance was decisively shaped by the philosophical and literary movement of humanism, which made the capabilities of the human individual its central concern. Humanism was a fundamental shift from the medieval dogma of understanding human nature from a religious point of view.

The sweeping intellectual changes that took place during the Renaissance prepared the way for the Scientific Revolution. In fact, modern scientific thought did not emerge with Galileo, as is usually stated by historians of science, but a century before with Leonardo da Vinci (1452–1519), the great genius of the Renaissance.

Leonardo is famous as an artist, engineer, and inventor of countless machines and mechanical devices, but his scientific work is still relatively unknown, despite his voluminous notebooks full of detailed descriptions of his experiments and long analyses of his findings. Leonardo developed a new empirical approach, involving the systematic observation of nature, reasoning, and mathematics—in other words, the main characteristics of what is known today as the scientific method. But his science was radically different from the mechanistic science that would emerge two hundred years later. It was a science of organic forms, qualities, and processes of transformation, which shows some striking parallels to our contemporary systems and complexity theories (see Chapter 5).[1]

Many aspects of Leonardo's science are still Aristotelian, but what makes it sound so modern to us today is that his forms are living forms, continually shaped and transformed by underlying processes. Throughout his life he studied, drew, and painted the rocks and sediments of the Earth, shaped by water; the growth of plants, shaped by their metabolism; and the anatomy of the animal body in motion. Nature as a whole was alive for Leonardo, and, like the earliest Greek philosophers, he saw the patterns and processes in the microcosm as being similar to those in the macrocosm.

In today's scientific parlance, we would call Leonardo a systemic thinker. Understanding a phenomenon, for him, meant connecting it with other phenomena through a similarity of patterns. When he studied the proportions of the human body, for instance, Leonardo compared them to the proportions of buildings in Renaissance architecture; his investigations of muscles and bones led him to study and draw gears and levers, thus interlinking animal physiology and engineering; patterns of turbulence in water led him to observe similar patterns in the flow of air; and from there he went on to explore the nature of sound, the theory of music, and the design of musical instruments. This exceptional ability to interconnect observations and ideas from different disciplines lies at the very heart of Leonardo's approach to learning and research.

Unlike most of his contemporaries, Leonardo rarely referred to God's creation, preferring instead to speak of the infinite works and marvelous inventions of nature. His notebooks are full of passages in which he describes how nature has "ordained" that animals should experience pain, how nature has created stones, given movement to animals, and formed their bodies. In all of these passages, one senses Leonardo's great reverence for nature's boundless creativity and wisdom.

Leonardo did not use the term "laws of nature." But, like subsequent generations of scientists, he did work from the basic premise that the physical universe is fundamentally ordered and that its causal relationships can be comprehended by the rational mind and expressed mathematically. He used the term *necessity* to express the stringent nature of those ordered causal relationships. Because his science was a science of qualities, of organic forms and their movements and transformations, the mathematical "necessity" he saw in nature was expressed not in quantities but in geometric shapes continually transforming themselves according to rigorous laws and principles. "Mathematical" for Leonardo referred above all to the logic, rigor, and coherence according to which nature has shaped, and is continually reshaping, its organic forms.

Leonardo did not pursue science and engineering in order to dominate nature, as Francis Bacon would advocate a century later, but always tried to learn as much as possible from nature. He was in awe of the beauty he saw in the complexity of natural forms, patterns, and processes, and aware that nature's ingenuity was far superior to human design. Accordingly, he often used natural processes and structures as models for his own designs.

THE SCIENTIFIC REVOLUTION

In the sixteenth and seventeenth centuries, the medieval worldview changed radically. The notion of an organic, living, spiritual universe was replaced by a view of the world as a machine, and this remained the dominant metaphor of the modern era until late in the twentieth century. The rise of this mechanistic worldview was brought about by revolutionary changes in physics and astronomy. Because of the crucial role of science in bringing about these far-reaching changes, historians have called the sixteenth and seventeenth centuries the age of the Scientific Revolution. It inaugurated the modern era, also known as "modernity."[2] This was also the time when the notion of "laws of nature" became firmly established in Western science.[3]

The Scientific Revolution began with Nicolaus Copernicus (1473–1543), who overthrew the geocentric view that placed the Earth at the center of the universe—a view that had been accepted dogma for more than a thousand years. Following him, Johannes Kepler (1571–1630) searched for the harmony of the spheres and was able, through painstaking work with astronomical tables, to formulate his celebrated empirical laws of planetary motion. These laws gave further support to the Copernican system. Kepler was the first to use the term *laws*, in accordance with the Aristotelian view that the celestial spheres were the realm of perfect mathematical laws. But the real change in scientific opinion was brought about by Galileo Galilei (1564–1642), who, with the help of the newly invented telescope, was able to discredit the old cosmology beyond any doubt. His striking astronomical discoveries—of the four moons of Jupiter; of the phases of Venus, which resemble the phases of the moon; and many others—established the Copernican hypothesis as a valid scientific theory.

In the terrestrial realm, Galileo experimented with falling bodies, which he was able to describe in mathematical terms. Galileo postulated that, in order to be effective in describing nature mathematically, scientists should restrict themselves to studying those properties of material bodies—shapes, numbers, and movement—that could be measured and quantified. Other properties, such as color, sound, taste, or smell, were merely subjective mental projections that should be excluded from the domain of science. He did not use the term *laws* for the mathematical regularities he discovered, but the new scientific strategy he proposed did open the door for describing the natural order in terms of the "laws of nature."

Galileo's strategy of directing scientists' attention to the quantifiable properties of matter proved extremely successful in physics, but it also exacted a heavy toll. During the centuries after Galileo, the focus on quantities was extended from the study of matter to the study of all natural and social phenomena, which prevented scientists for several centuries from understanding many essential properties of life.

While Galileo devised ingenious experiments in Italy, Francis Bacon (1561–1626) explicitly set forth the empirical method of science in England. Bacon formulated a clear theory of the inductive procedure: to make experiments and to draw conclusions from them, which could then be tested by further experiments. He became extremely influential by vigorously advocating his new method. The "Baconian spirit," as it was called, profoundly changed the nature and purpose of the scientific quest. From the time of the ancients, the goal of natural philosophy had been to achieve wisdom—to understand the natural order and live in harmony with it. In the seventeenth century, however, this attitude changed dramatically. As the organic view of nature was replaced by the metaphor of the world as a machine, the goal of science became a quest for knowledge that could be used to dominate and control nature. Henceforth, the Earth would no longer be seen as a nurturing mother but as a resource to be exploited without limits.

THE NEWTONIAN WORLD-MACHINE AND
THE CONCEPTION OF THE LAWS OF NATURE

The shift from the organic to the mechanistic worldview was initiated by one of the major figures of the seventeenth century, René Descartes (1596–1650). Descartes is usually regarded as the founder of modern philosophy, but he was also a brilliant mathematician and a very influential scientist. He developed a new method of reasoning, which he presented in his most famous book, *Discourse on the Method of Rightly Conducting One's Reason and of Seeking Truth in the Sciences*. Although this text has become one of the great philosophical classics, its original purpose was not to teach philosophy but to serve as an introduction to science.

Descartes's method is analytic and was designed to reach scientific truth. It consists of breaking up thoughts and problems into pieces and then arranging these pieces in their logical order.

This method is useful in many ways, but in subsequent centuries an overemphasis on the Cartesian method led to the fragmentation that is characteristic of both our general thinking and our academic disciplines. The Cartesian method has also led to the widespread attitude of reductionism in science—the belief that all aspects of complex phenomena can be understood by reducing them to their smallest constituent parts.

Descartes based his view of nature on a fundamental division between two independent, separate, and essentially different realms: that of mind, or *res cogitans* (the "thinking thing"), and that of matter, or *res extensa* (the "extended thing"). The material universe was a machine for Descartes, and nothing but a machine. Nature worked according to mechanical laws, and everything in the material world, both living and nonliving, could be explained in terms of the arrangement and movement of its parts.

Descartes claimed that the only difference between artificial and natural bodies was one of size. In artifacts made by craftspeople, the machines are large and visible, whereas in nature they are small and often invisible, but the motion of a clock is in principle no different from the growth of a tree. Descartes also extended this comparison to the human body: "I consider the human body as a machine," he wrote.[4] "My thought compares a sick man and an ill-made clock with my idea of a healthy man and a well-made clock." This mechanical picture of nature became the dominant paradigm of science in subsequent centuries.

Descartes was also the first to give the term "laws of nature" a central place within natural philosophy. He proposed three principles of how the states of motion of material bodies were conserved and transmitted, and he described these as "certain rules, which I call the laws of nature."[5] Descartes's first and second laws state that a body at rest will remain at rest, and a body in motion will move in a straight line with constant speed unless something external intervenes. These rules were later restated by Newton and are now known as Newton's first law of motion. Descartes's third law describes colliding bodies; this law contains several flaws because he did not have a clear conception of what we now call the conservation of momentum. Nonetheless, Descartes reserved the term "law" for those three principles. No other theorem, rule, or principle was called a law in his system. Following the custom of medieval philosophy, still widespread in his time, Descartes invoked theological reasons for his three laws of nature, founding them on the immutability of God and his operations.

In England, the terminology came to be used more often. The founding of the Royal Society in 1660 for the purpose of promoting the new mechanistic science attracted considerable public attention, and suspicions of atheism were raised. To defend themselves against such accusations, the Fellows of the Royal Society found it convenient to adopt Descartes's language of the "laws of nature" and its implied association with a divine legislator. They extended this terminology widely, speaking of mechanical laws, laws of motion, optical laws, laws of magnetism, and so forth.

The culmination of mechanistic science and of the concept of the "laws of nature" came with Isaac Newton (1642–1727). Newton developed a complete mathematical formulation of the mechanistic view of nature, and thus accomplished a grand synthesis of the works of Copernicus, Kepler, Galileo, Bacon, and Descartes. Newtonian physics, the crowning achievement of seventeenth-century science, provided a consistent mathematical theory of the world that remained the solid foundation of scientific thought until the twentieth century.

Newton published his theory in 1687 in his celebrated *Philosophiae Naturalis Principia Mathematica*, in which he put forth "axioms, or laws of motion" as well as the law of gravitation, the law of refraction, and other laws. From that time on, the notion of laws of nature became firmly established not only in England but also in France, where scientists had been reluctant to use the term before. In fact, many of the great discoveries of the seventeenth century, which their authors had not expressed in terms of "laws," were given that name later on, such as Galileo's law of falling bodies, Willebrord Snell's (1580–1626) law of refraction, or Blaise Pascal's (1623–1662) law of the distribution of pressure.

Newtonian mechanics was tremendously successful in the eighteenth and nineteenth centuries. The Newtonian theory explained the motion of the planets, moons, and comets down to the smallest detail, as well as the flow of the tides and various other phenomena related to gravity. Newton's mathematical system of the world—with his law of gravity and his three laws of motion at its center—quickly established itself as the correct theory of physical reality and generated enormous enthusiasm among scientists and the lay public alike. Newton became the archetypal scientific genius, not unlike Albert Einstein in the twentieth century.

Encouraged by the brilliant success of Newtonian mechanics in astronomy, physicists extended his principles far beyond the description of macroscopic bodies. The behaviors of solids, liquids, and gases, including the phenomena of heat and sound, were explained successfully in terms of the motion of elementary material particles. In the nineteenth century, chemists developed a precise atomic theory of chemistry that paved the way for the conceptual unification of physics and chemistry in the twentieth century. And again scientists repeatedly formulated the regularities they observed in chemical interactions in terms of "laws."

Thus, for scientists of the eighteenth and nineteenth centuries, the tremendous success of the mechanistic model confirmed their belief that the universe was a huge mechanical system, running according to the Newtonian laws of motion, and that Newton's mechanics was the ultimate theory of natural phenomena. Gone was the time-honored conception of the universe as an ordered, harmonious, living whole. In its place was a view of a universe made of pieces that could be broken apart, studied, quantified, and reordered according to need. As we shall see, this mechanistic view also had a significant impact on a very different kind of law— human law—the effects of which are still with us today.

CHAPTER 3

From Commons to Capital

The Evolution of Western Legal Thought

The fundamental transformation in science that produced the mechanistic approach and its notion of the laws of nature finds striking parallels in the development of Western legal thought. Just as scientific thinkers following Galileo, Descartes, and Newton divided the whole into an aggregate of separate parts governed by strict laws of nature, legal scientists fragmented the medieval legal order, a holistic system that had adapted customary religious and Roman law materials to the practical requirements of flesh-and-blood human relationships. In the transition to modernity, Western legal scholars began to conceive of the law as an aggregate of discrete component parts governed by strict natural laws of individual reason. The ancient holistic vision of the world as a *kósmos*, of the Earth as a generous gift of God to humankind as a whole and abundant commonwealth collectively accessible by all, was replaced by a humanist emphasis on the individual and human reason, which resulted in a mechanistic legal vision known as rationalist natural law.[1]

Legal humanists prepared the intellectual foundations for a dramatic transformation from commons-based folk legal institutions into legally formalized, concentrated private property and eventually into capital. Private ownership—individual dominion over land—became the most important legal concept, dividing the whole into individualistic components. The mechanism governing the relationship between these parts was found in what became the sovereign state.

Like the transformation in science, the movement from legal wholeness to the modern, Western vision of law grounded in individual ownership and state sovereignty lasted several centuries, and the intellectual legal path was complex, because religion, law, science, and philosophy were not neatly severable from one another. Indeed, sometimes one theorist would work in what we today consider completely different areas of knowledge—for example, Francis Bacon's work spanned law and science. And although legal systems in the Continental tradition (known as civil law) and those in the English tradition (known as common law) spring from different legal origins, both systems ultimately are rooted in ancient Roman law and share the fundamental legal ideology that dominates the world today.[2]

ROMAN ABSOLUTE OWNERSHIP

Ancient Greece contributed far more to Western political thought than to Western legal tradition. Aristotle's comments on human laws, for instance, were rather cursory and were disseminated across various works. Still, he introduced some fundamental legal distinctions that have survived until today, such as the idea that law can be customary or enacted, written or unwritten. Private property also occupies a central position in Aristotle's social thought. He vigorously defended private property as an institution legitimized by reason and leading to virtue. This defense was presented in opposition to Plato's ideal of communal property, which Plato articulated as a way to guarantee the detachment of the ruling elite from worldly, material concerns.[3]

In general, however, the remote origins of the Western legal tradition are found not in ancient Greece but in ancient Rome, where the process of resolving disputes among peers gave birth to a professionalized legal tradition.[4] According to both its origin myth and current scholarly knowledge, Rome at its founding (ca. 750 B.C.E.) covered a relatively small territory around the river Tiber, which its first king, Romulus, divided among the men who had taken part in the founding of the new city. Each of these patriarchal family heads received an allotment of land where he enjoyed absolute power over whatever he brought there, including his family members and his slaves. Moreover, just as Romulus had the absolute power to exclude anybody from the boundaries of the new city (a power that he famously exercised by killing his twin brother, who challenged him), every patriarch was empowered to exclude anybody from the perimeter of his private land.

To avoid armed conflicts arising from possible disputes about the boundaries of land or other contentious questions, the original patriarchs met in an assembly of peers, the Senate, to discuss important common issues such as defense, political organization, or economic needs. The maintenance of social peace among these decentralized sovereigns was crucial, and therefore legal institutions were created early on to protect the respective boundaries of their properties. Private ownership became the foundational building block of the Roman legal organization.

However, the extraordinary contribution of Roman law to the Western legal tradition lies not so much in its recognition of private property, which was already recognized in Greece and in many other places, but in its formalization of a professionalized legal system capable of defining and enforcing proprietary interests—on land as well as on other things—in great detail.[5] This system represented a significant change from earlier folk legal traditions on the Italian peninsula and elsewhere.

In pastoral or semi-pastoral societies—such as pre-Roman society, or even today in remote villages in such places as Afghanistan, Yemen, Somalia, Mali, or Andean regions where similar patriarchal systems can still be found—most land is held in common and used according to the needs of semi-nomadic people. In such conditions of decentralized power, the solution of property conflicts is crucial to the survival of the village or society. However, traditional solutions are not understood as a professionally managed affair in which one individual litigant is "right" and wins, while the other is "wrong" and loses. People understand that they will still need to live together after the issue is resolved. Thus, most often the solution is to seek accommodation among groups. Instead of enforcing the compliance of one party with a formalized, preexisting system of legal rules described by a specialized legal profession, decisions are made with an eye toward future relationships. ✳

Such mechanisms for resolving communal disputes are the most antique institutions, and certainly the more-or-less sedentary populations inhabiting the Italian peninsula since Neolithic times had developed ways to solve disputes other than through armed conflict. But Roman law represented a break with this tradition. Even if Rome was from the very beginning, as some modern archaeologists think, the outcome of an incremental aggregation of pastoral households, it did not function like any bottom-up aggregation of patriarchal sovereign owners. It developed an urban legal system, concerned with property as a political institution belonging exclusively to patriarchs—though property owners still enjoyed access to surrounding non-owned rural commons.

Over time in Rome a legal distinction arose about things that were not strictly private property: "things belonging to nobody" (*res nullius*), everything that could be owned but actually was not, which could be freely occupied; "things belonging to everyone" (*res communis omnium*), such as air, sea, beaches, and running water that could not by their nature be owned based on the principle of exclusion; and "things belonging to the city" (*res publicae*), public land, squares, aqueducts, or sewers. The enforcement of these distinctions, which were never clear-cut but always blurred over time and space, was put under the responsibility of an administrator. First in the city—where the surrounding non-owned rural commons were incrementally privatized by large slave-holding rural farms—and later across a huge, conquered empire, this legal technique made the Romans capable of solving issues of coexistence in such a way that each issue could be solved according to a pre-established legal rule, rooted in individualized absolute ownership, and would lead to a similar, subsequent solution.

We see here the roots of a formalized, professionalized concept of the law. During the Roman Republic (beginning around 510 B.C.E.), these early institutions evolved into complex legal structures. The Senate granted a large amount of administrative power

to the *praetor*, an elected politician who, among many other func-
tions, including the maintenance of public property, was responsible for resolving private conflicts, generally about property and
its limits. Prospective plaintiffs brought complaints to the praetor,
who then appointed another citizen (a Roman peer) to serve as a
lay *iudex*—a kind of one-man jury—and instructed him about the
law to be applied in deciding who had acted within the limits of
his property rights and who had transgressed them or intruded on
the rights of someone else.

In practice, however, the praetor had neither the time nor the
skills to reduce complex factual situations into a plain issue for the
iudex to decide according to the law. In fact, by the time of the Republic, edicts and other enacted laws limiting citizens' power had
already accumulated, becoming quite numerous and complex, so
that neither praetor nor *iudex* had any real knowledge about them.
Therefore, the praetor appointed private individuals to help with
these complex legal tasks. These were usually wealthy patricians
(the aristocratic, landed class) who had made the study of the law
their hobby. Through a skillful study of precedents, edicts, and
the opinions of their peers, they prepared instructions to the *iudex*
called *formulae*. Over time, small and highly influential schools of
jurists developed and kept track of the formulas that were to be
used over and over again. This became a highly professionalized
system of law, grounded in real, practical conflicts—again, mostly
among property-owning citizens.

In the second century C.E., a little-known teacher of law, Gaius,
who was most likely a slave, attempted for the first time to give a
systematic order to these brief legal texts. He organized them into
a short booklet on Roman law called the *Institutiones*.[6] His definition of law—"The law is what the people order and establish"—is
exceptionally modern. Gaius divided the whole legal universe into
laws related to persons, laws related to property, and laws related
to actions. The common feature of these three types of laws—individual owners acting in their own self-interest against other individuals—has remained the archetype of Western law to this day.

During subsequent centuries, Roman law evolved through the

process of resolving many individual conflicts, increasing in complexity with the development of social activity. Eventually the juristic opinions, derived from imperial enactments and refinements of previous formulas, became overly complicated and often mutually contradictory, resulting in legal disorder rather than a legal order. Emperor Justinian (ca. 482–565) decreed that the whole body of law should be restated, simplified, rationalized, and then enacted once and for all by himself, as the supreme lawgiver of the Roman Empire. This compilation, completed in 534 c.e., was the *Corpus iuris civilis* (Body of Civil Law), also known as the Code of Justinian.

The text represents the first attempt to create a complete body of law by design, professionally organized around the power and prerogatives of individual owners, and granted the force of law by the power of the ruler. It also provides the conceptual foundation for our present-day property-centered vision of the law, which evolved from it over the subsequent centuries. For this reason alone, Justinian's *Corpus iuris* remains the most important law book ever written, the foundational book of the Western legal tradition.[7]

THE RISE OF LEGAL PROFESSIONALISM

With the death of Justinian (565 c.e.) and of his dream to reunify the Roman Empire, the Code declined in authority and eventually was physically lost shortly after its promulgation. At the dawn of the eleventh century, it mysteriously reappeared in a library near Pisa, where someone found a copy. It quickly became the foundational text for law teaching in the oldest western university, which had been established in Bologna in 1088. This second, academic, life of the Roman law was, of course, no longer backed by the long-disappeared imperial power. Instead, as jurists like to say, it ruled by "power of reason" (*imperio rationis*) rather than by "reason of power" (*ratione imperii*). In Continental Europe professional jurists still provided the intellectual power behind its development and transformation, but instead of helping to adjudicate cases they were active in academic teaching and research. Through their work, Roman law, progressively adapted to new circumstances, became the general law of Continental Europe, providing a shared Latin-language basis for building new institutions in city-states, municipalities, kingdoms, and newly established empires. In their hands, Roman law became a coherent whole, consistent with the needs of a largely pluralistic medieval society.[8]

The jurist Irnerius (1050–1125), author of the first glosses and commentaries on the rediscovered Code, formed the School of Glossators at the University of Bologna late in the eleventh century. The Code provided the textual basis for teaching law, much as the Bible was the authoritative text for the medieval schools of theology. Thus, the Continental legal tradition, in the absence of robust centralized political institutions, originated and unfolded in an academic setting.

These early legal scholars were primarily interested in understanding the literal meaning of the *Corpus iuris civilis*. The text contained a large number of old Roman factual situations and legal opinions related to those situations, with no easily detectable patterns or principles. Just glossing the text—writing an explanation of its literal meaning—and reproducing the annotated text in an increasing number of copies was a highly commendable and sophisticated intellectual activity. A class of lawyers conversant with the Roman texts soon developed; they were to occupy important posts in late medieval and early modern political institutions.

By 1230, Franciscus Accursius (1182–1260), an academic jurist of French origin active in Bologna, had essentially completed the glossing work; he assembled his own and thousands of earlier glosses into an exhaustive compilation known as the *Glossa ordinaria*. Bartolus of Saxoferrato (1313–1357), the outstanding medieval jurist and intellectual, together with his disciples, produced a more principled and coherent commentary. This academic commentary on Justinian law worked as the common law of the European continent, and, thus transformed, Roman law became the authoritative text for the teaching of civil law both on the Continent and at the universities of Oxford and Cambridge in England.

(As discussed below, the English legal tradition developed in the practice of early courts of law as judicial power became centralized under the Plantagenet sovereigns.)

In the countryside, the law governing the everyday life of ordinary people almost everywhere remained customary folk law, which governed the peasants' life as it had for centuries. Thus, the most formidable impact of the spread of Roman legal thought was in framing the fundamental legal ideas of the ruling class, including the Roman Catholic Church, which always deployed legally trained clergy to organize itself as a powerful hierarchy. The position of property ownership, grounded in a fundamental vision of private, individual rights, with collective obligations progressively transferred from the community (*res communis*) to its centralized political institutions (*res publicae*), remained very strong among these early professional jurists.

Roman property owners, and later Roman consuls and emperors, had violently expanded their domains by privatizing resources held in common, and jurists promptly dubbed these resources *res nullius* (belonging to nobody) to justify their privatization. Suddenly, things belonging to everyone, including ordinary peasants' access to commons, in fact belonged to no one—no one had legal title over them as private property. They were up for grabs. The imposition of centralized authority and power over natural resources—whether this authority was public or private—was an early subtraction of those resources from the undivided commonwealth. Previously, this commonwealth had been governed by customs and folk law that, at least in theory, could protect access to it. Now, what was primarily protected was someone's power to exclude others from such access.[9]

ENCLOSURE AND THE LEGALIZED EROSION OF THE COMMONS

A similar phenomenon characterized the origins of the common-law tradition in medieval England.[10] The process of academic legal development that affected the European continent did not cross the Channel to England. Instead, beginning around the time of the Norman conquest (1066), the early centralized Royal Courts at Westminster Hall in London developed the common law of the kingdom through their judicial decisions. The common-law tradition emerged after the Norman conquest as a system of rules to solve proprietary conflicts among landed gentry. The Magna Carta of 1215 challenged the fiction that all land belongs to the king and protected the power of the landed individual (in this case, the barons).

The Norman kings of England and their tenants-in-chief had been expanding their power by constant attempts to privatize commons, sometimes fighting among each other in the process, and more rarely being defeated by communities resisting such seizures. While the Magna Carta gave the barons' property rights constitutional protection against the king, the lesser-known Charter of the Forest was issued in 1217 to protect the common right of ordinary people to the forest—against both the king and the barons.[11] Despite its subsequent burial under thousands of pages of legal commentary that focused only on private property protection, the Charter of the Forest represented an early, though failed, attempt to protect peasants' equal access to nature and its gifts of water, food, fuel, and shelter, against centralized extractive control, both private (by the barons) and public (by the king). In subsequent centuries, the private enclosure of the vast English commons, justified through the power to exclude and guaranteed by the tort of trespass, became the best-known instance of the transformation of the commons into private property.

In talking about resources, it is important to remember that most of the resources needed for the satisfaction of human wants are not created but are extracted, that is, taken from nature. Humans cannot create even a simple resource such as water, nor can we, in its absence, produce any food. The control and accumulation of resources for future consumption was and remains a key element of political tension and the principal motivation for human institutional development.

The transformations that led to the rise of Western modernity required the extraction, accumulation, and mobilization of staggering amounts of natural and human resources, later to be understood as "capital."[12] During the sixteenth and seventeenth centuries, legal innovations coherent with the new spirit of the time were introduced to obtain the kind of power and economic concentration that was needed for the modern state to establish itself as a sovereign, imperialistic power capable of reaching newly discovered lands abroad. For instance, the growing English textile industry required the ability to graze sheep in large quantity to supply wool, which in turn led to a need to fence in land previously in common use and customarily kept accessible by medieval common law.

To be sure, the usurpation of peasants' rights of access to land was neither new nor limited to England; as we have seen, the usurpation had also been characteristic of the Roman power holders. Nevertheless, the intensity of the process of transforming common land into private property, which began in the late fifteenth century and was completed by the early nineteenth century, has no precedent in history. Nor was there a precedent for the complex process of transforming of the law to accommodate the annihilation of customary rights such as gleaning, collection of wood and other forest products, access to rivers and lakes, and so on.

Scholars are divided on the causes, consequences, and shifting attitudes of power holders toward the fencing of land in England. The Tudor kings and queens, fearing peasant unrest, resisted enclosure and passed legislation against it, in defiance of pro-enclosure gentry represented in Parliament. Nevertheless, acts of Parliament (known as the parliamentary enclosures) forced the privatization and the titling of land as private property after the overthrow of King James II in 1688 (known as the Glorious Revolution).

Revolts against enclosures, most famously the Midland Revolt in 1607, were frequent and bloody. Notions of land improvement and scientific agriculture were deployed during eighteenth-century debates about the desirability of enclosures, with agronomists, lawyers, economists, engineers, and even the philosopher John Locke busy working to transform a brutal class plunder against the poor into a narrative of progress and efficiency.[13] By the early nineteenth century, common lands accessible to all and governed by ancient customs had been relegated to remote mountain areas.

In some ways, those in favor of the massive enclosure movement were correct: enclosure, achieved through parliamentary legislation, was instrumental in the birth and development of textile manufacture, and largely explains England's role as the cradle of the Industrial Revolution. A centralized political system, put into practice in England before anywhere else, resulted from the "scientific" separation between public sovereignty and private property and created the best conditions for capitalism to develop its power and ideology. The resulting unprecedented concentration of capital, along with scientific advances, produced the spectacular technological successes of the early part of the eighteenth century.[14]

This success came with a great cost. Most peasants who had previously been engaged in subsistence agriculture, guaranteed by access to the commons, were dispossessed and excluded from the rapidly rationalized agricultural production. Although many of them were needed for work in early concentrated manufacturing, they often resisted displacement, urbanization, and factory life. Thus, the roaming poor became a social problem for early modern England.

No one has described the effects of enclosure better than the humanist Sir Thomas More (1478–1535), himself a very accomplished lawyer and chancellor of the early Courts of Equity. In his best-known book, *Utopia*, More vividly described the process in the early days of the enclosure movement:

> Your sheep, which are naturally mild, . . . may be said now to devour men and unpeople, not only villages, but towns; for wherever it is found that the sheep of any soil yield a softer and richer wool than ordinary, there the nobility and gentry, and even those holy men, the abbots, not contented with the old rents . . . stop the course of agriculture . . . and enclose grounds that they may lodge their sheep in them . . . those worthy countrymen turn the best inhabited places into solitudes . . . the owners, as well as tenants, are turned out of their possessions by trick or by main force, or, being wearied out by ill usage, they are forced to sell them.[15]

Although the enclosure movement was promoted with abundant literature on "agricultural improvement," it is better understood as a fundamental, though often turbulent, agreement between the interests of the Crown (championed by Lord Chancellor Francis Bacon) and those of the landed aristocracy (championed by Chief Justice Sir Edward Coke [1552–1634]) to dismantle all the guarantees of the Charter of the Forest.

THE DEAL BETWEEN SOVEREIGNTY AND OWNERSHIP

Following the Glorious Revolution, the Act of Settlement (1701) not only arranged the succession to the English and Irish thrones but also, very importantly, established the principle of the "rule of law" as a scientific truth. Common-law judges received tenure of office during good behavior. Thus they were equipped to guarantee private property against any sovereign encroachment, which was limited by "due process of law"; sovereign power was to be respectful of both common law and the statutes interpreted by the courts.[16] Henceforth, professionally trained lawyers would decide which process was *due*, discovering and declaring the law of the land with the help of the scientific method taught by Bacon. Judges, subject only to the law (declared by themselves), would also resolve conflicts of prerogative between the Parliament (representing property) and the Crown (representing sovereignty).

The Act of Settlement, however, completely excluded the commons and the political forces representing them. It did not allow for any serious judicial scrutiny of the enclosure process, because commoners and peasants, lacking parliamentary representation, had no access to the courts. In general, courts of law were (and remain) ill equipped to protect collective interests, especially of the poor. Thus, this compromise known as the rule of law not only dispossessed masses of peasants but also provided all sorts of legal means, often highly cruel and full of fantasy, to force the dispossessed to work in the service of the new machinery of property concentration: the manufacturing industry.[17]

Thus the rule of law stripped the commons from the domain

of interests protected by law. Indeed, quite a number of collective rights recognized by the medieval feudal tenure system, described and administered by Coke, ultimately disappeared following the triumph of unrestricted modern private property, championed by Bacon and Locke. The very intensive and effective dominant propaganda about the improvement produced by modernity makes it hard to approach medieval law with a minimum of detached historical awareness.[18] Yet in general, the enclosure of the commons not only divided the land but also separated humans from the *kósmos* and divided whole communities into discrete parts. People who had once been members of a community now found themselves largely alone in an unfriendly urban environment. This major shift replaced a lifestyle (which was certainly very hard) in which peasants were a component part of their ecological community with a lifestyle (perhaps even harder) of labor in exchange for a salary.

The transformation of peasants into industrial workers involved much more than just forcing a traditionally exploited class into a new trade. The peasant life, supported by guaranteed common resources and the simple collective institutions of the commons, was hard, but not alienating. Peasants worked when the weather allowed them to do so and typically spent much time cooperating with each other in building, cooking, or producing food. When the dark or the cold would not allow outside work, they spent time together indoors, attending to different occupations. Despite a variety of vexations that affected the conditions of peasants under the medieval feudal system, commoners in a village economy enjoyed a unity of life and labor, and life was not repetitive. In general, the average person's existence, though certainly short (though not necessarily shorter than in town), was quality-based and relational in its nature; it was not a quantified unit of time to be sold on the market. *Challenges concept of money, property, & the like.*

Life in such commons-based organic communities was difficult for an outside authority to organize, discipline, or rationalize. The law of the commons comprised reciprocal duties between the individual and the community and long-term relationships. It was a local system, lacking formal courts and any distinction between legal, religious, and political authority. Medieval folk law governing access to and use of the commons was an often-contested but always negotiated human institution, highly adaptable to the circumstances of each conflict and thus impossible to describe before the fact. Overall, the goals were inclusion and community rather than exclusion and individualization; tradition promoted the diffusion of responsibility and social duties rather than the accumulation and concentration of power.

One of the longest-lasting effects of legal modernization was to "outlaw" this model of social organization. Although these local, highly context-specific, pluralistic variations were endowed with tremendous flexibility and great capacity to hold communities together, they were not considered "real law" by the members of the legal profession—judges, barristers, attorneys, and scholars. Indeed, this social organization opposed the two winning institutions of modernity, private property and state sovereignty, which worked together to dismantle this traditional system and transform people and resources into capital.

Factory conditions were highly repetitive, and neither the weather nor the season mattered. The working experience, rather than being improved when more community members joined in, was actually made worse by the quantity of available labor, which enabled owners to pay lower wages and maintain poor working conditions. When peasants resisted this new, alienating form of earning a living, state authorities were prepared to provide the owners of the means of production with the force necessary to enforce this new, "rational" system of work and commerce. Laws harshly punished vagabonds, the poor, and the unemployed. Prisons and mental hospitals, which had never been needed in rural settings where the community would effectively police deviants with the threat of ostracism, were invented at the end of the eighteenth century as an integral part of this process.[19]

As humanism put forth individual reason as the foundation of modern society, the organic community was defamed as a symbol of collective oppression over the individual and the medieval commons were denounced as places of no law, only of ignorance. Modern, legal institutions based on individual property rights successfully replaced the medieval holistic vision. The conception of the world as created by God and the common property of all was replaced with that of a fragmented land in which individual owners in competition with one another controlled all resources. In subsequent centuries, legal and political scientists following this humanistic vision and the supposed purity of Roman antiquity have denied any legal legitimacy to any human organizations that operate outside of the reductionist dualism of private property and state sovereignty. One narrative only has become dominant, in which human progress is described as a progressive exit from a brutal state of nature into a world where people dominate nature and adapt it to human needs. Even today, the commons are at the mercy of the government in office, treated as the property of the sovereign state and not of the people; as such, the commons can be freely sold or privatized (that is, taken from our common wealth) without judicial scrutiny of any kind.[20]

THE INTERPLAY OF SCIENCE AND LAW: FRANCIS BACON

As we have seen, Francis Bacon was both a natural philosopher and an experienced practitioner of the law. As one of the creators of the scientific canon and as a champion of the monarchy in the struggle that led eventually to the 1701 Act of Settlement, seventy-five years after his death, his legal and political views were shaped by his scientific outlook. No author helps us to better understand the abyss between legal knowledge, based on ancient formalisms and legitimized by custom, and modern scientific knowledge, with its claim of being based on clear, measurable laws of nature.[21] Bacon was the first English lawyer to engage in what we could call a total critique of the common-law tradition; he was also the first to draw an explicit analogy between the concept of the laws of nature and the legal realm.

In discussing the law, Bacon distinguished between "habits of nature," observed in specific regions, and "fundamental and common laws," which could be discovered and viewed as a background for these local variations. One dimension of law is customary and highly mutable from place to place; another dimension is professionalized, common, and potentially scientific. The latter, called common law in the Anglo-American tradition, has been the province of jurists since the initial formation of Roman law. Nevertheless, in Bacon's time it was judges, not scholars, who were in charge of declaring the common laws of England, and Bacon considered their methods to be medieval and unscientific—particularly in comparison with his most advanced contemporaries, the academic legal humanists who were teaching Roman law according to the most advanced scientific standards of the time, both in England and on the Continent.

Bacon considered the common-law tradition to be a collection of medieval formalisms, based on ignorance and superstition and serving the political interests of the landed aristocracy. Medieval law included rituals, symbols, and magical beliefs as well as subjective intellectual interpretations. In this system, an oath could be considered proof, and the various rituals to ascertain the truth might include anything from trial by battle to ordeal by water or fire, where God was the ultimate decision maker. Though rarely applied in Bacon's time, these evidentiary devices were still available in the catalogue of acceptable legal forms; in Bacon's time and much later, they helped to determine the legal strategy in litigation. The writ of trespass (an action to recover damages against someone who voluntarily invaded someone's property), for example, developed as the most expansive form of private ownership protection because it was tried by jury. This was a much more rational device than the the trial by battle of horses used in the writ of right, the legal device traditionally designed for protecting the owner. The more rational procedure made plaintiffs favor trespass even if the writ of right would have allowed them to obtain a specific remedy not limited to pecuniary compensation as in trespass.[22]

The medieval common law of property, famously described in the most important law book of Bacon's time, Coke's *Institutes* (known as Coke upon Littleton), also included customs, uses, manners, ethics, religion, and, ultimately, politics. Such were the "irrationalities" that legal modernity, pioneered by Bacon, was trying to ban from its rational laws by design. Just as taste, scent, color, and beauty had been banned from scientific inquiry, so too were customs, ethics, values, justice, morals, manners, and sentiments—everything that gives life to the law—eventually banned from the absolutist vision of the legal order. This vision, now known as legal positivism, still dominates law today.

Bacon was intimately familiar with the inquisitorial procedure, which included "torture of the truth" out of a defendant, because these procedures applied in the Courts of Chancery. As part of his attempt to modernize the writ system that still dominated common-law procedures, therefore, Bacon produced many changes, especially in the rules of evidence. Bacon streamlined and made scientific the legal procedures used to search for the truth. For the first time—and this was a massive improvement— legal scholars began to consider that factual inquiry, in the form of historical research about the events that generated the litigation, was necessary to the application of any legal sanction. Likewise, the procedure in Bacon's Court of Chancery could be initiated very simply, through a complaint and issuance of a summons, just as it happens today, and would proceed with discovery devices remarkably modern and similar to those contained in the American Federal Rules of Civil Procedure.

It is not possible to know whether it was Bacon the lawyer who affected Bacon the scientist with his idea of torturing nature to extract its secrets,[23] or if Bacon the scientist influenced the law reformer to get rid of formalisms incompatible with the inquiry into truth. In any event, through Bacon, the Anglo-American law of evidence inherited the idea that direct rational inquiry could bring to light factual truth in a reliable and final way. Thus, the spirit of the Scientific Revolution, especially in the form of Cartesian rationalism, was deeply absorbed into legal theory and was embedded in the institutional settings of human law by Europe's leading jurists.

FROM HOLISTIC TO ANTHROPOCENTRIC NATURAL LAW

In the movement toward privatizing the commons, a crucial intellectual strategy was the transformation of natural law from a system legitimized by God into a system legitimized by human reason. This movement required getting rid of the ancient and medieval ideas of holism and unity that had dominated lawyers' thinking. Holism, a vision of reality in which religion, natural philosophy, politics, and law are understood as a seamless whole, characterized the thought of the fourteenth century. It defined the academic synthesis of Roman legal materials provided by Bartolus of Saxoferrato, which remained the canon in the common law of Europe for centuries to come. In England, two hundred years later, holism pervaded the synthesis of the common law by Coke, who remained extraordinarily influential in spite of Bacon's critique.

During the sixteenth century, holism was still the dominant vision of the leading school of jurisprudence of the time, the late Spanish scholastics. Mostly active at the University of Salamanca, they were developing a comprehensive system known as Spanish natural law. The leaders of this school, such as Francisco de Vitoria (1492–1546), were the first jurists in the Western legal tradition to attempt an ambitious synthesis of Roman law with the ideas of Aristotle and Thomas Aquinas, much as Aquinas had earlier worked to fuse Aristotle's ideas with Christian theology.[24] The Spanish scholastics' highly organized system of natural law was designed to explain human laws within a holistic theory of God and nature, a grand vision that included a synthesis between the Aristotelian concepts of distributive and commutative justice. In Aristotle, distributive justice, which concerns the just distribution of goods in society, pertains to the whole, whereas commutative justice, concerned with the fulfillment of contractual obligations between individuals, pertains to the parts.[25]

The scholastic concern with distributive justice and thus the organic well-being of society continued to view the human as part of a holistic community. The humanistic spirit of the time, however, injected into this vision an unprecedented degree of concern with the rational individual as an "atom" of society, capable of finding its way within itself and not simply as a member of an all-pervasive collectivity. Sixteenth-century social and legal studies, developing in academic settings, could not long resist the movement toward examining society as an algebraic sum of its component parts. The new man did not need God, and especially not the Church, in his inquiry into the laws of nature. Likewise, inquiry into natural law required nothing more than human reason.

The late Spanish scholastics were the last learned medieval jurists on the Continent, and the equilibrium between the whole and the parts, which characterized their system of natural law, was the last example of organic medieval thought, though it was remarkably scientific in its method. Eventually, however, the most interesting holistic aspects of their vision were completely erased in the further development of natural law, whose rationalist form was developed after the Reformation in seventeenth-century Holland, mostly at the University of Leiden.

The decisive change came with Hugo Grotius (de Groot) (1583–1645), a Dutch Protestant lawyer and politician who founded what is known as the northern school of natural law, which was based on a Cartesian vision of rational natural laws. In this school of thought, natural law was reduced to a system of relationships between distinct sovereigns (physical or moral persons; the latter is a legal term for something like a state or a corporation) governed by a common law based on reason.[26] Grotius also laid the foundations of modern international law by asserting that the relationship between sovereigns either can be voluntary (by treaty) or can be governed by principles of "just war" waged by a legitimate sovereign, a notion he inherited from the Spanish scholastics.

For most of his life, Grotius worked as a hired gun serving the interests of the Dutch East India Company, the first global corporation. He demonstrated a staggering capacity to deduct from objective, universal principles of reason legal solutions that favored his powerful corporate clients yet remained acceptable to "civilized" sovereign nations.[27] Of special importance was Grotius's ability to offer legal advantages to private corporations over states.

For instance, in his book *Mare Liberum* (The Free Sea), he argued in favor of the East India Company's right to attack and plunder a Portuguese ship. Grotius argued that Portugal's claim of exclusivity on certain routes on the high seas was against the natural openness of this "global common," thus justifying the attack as actually protecting the rational order. Thus the discipline of international law was born in an act of corporate plunder, paradoxically justified by a brilliant jurist deploying the Roman legal concept of the high seas as a natural common (*res communis omnium*).

THE AGE OF REASON

The rationalist version of natural law that Grotius developed from the Cartesian paradigm was extended beyond international law by Samuel Pufendorf (1632–1694) in Germany and by the influential French jurist Jean Domat (1625–1696) in France. Another German philosopher, Christian Wolff (1679–1754), attempted to explain the fundamental principles of law in mathematical terms. Thus, in just one generation, natural law became equated with rationalism throughout Europe.

William Blackstone (1723–1780), the first law professor to teach English law at Oxford, offered the best-known natural-law definition of private property as the "sole and despotic dominion which one man claims and exercises over the external things of the world, in total exclusion of the right of any other individual in the universe" in his highly influential *Commentaries on the Laws of England* (1765–1769). This book, deeply influenced by Grotius, eventually replaced Coke's treatise as the most authoritative book on the common-law tradition. Blackstone's definition makes explicit the owner-centric idea of Western jurisprudence and demonstrates how the model of domination of the individual over nature had become naturalized by his time. Moreover, it shows a remarkable Cartesian influence in assuming an ontological separation between the despotic owner (comparable to Descartes's *res cogitans*) and the external world (*res extensa*).

During the eighteenth century, the belief in the rational approach to human problems spread so rapidly among Europe's middle classes that the whole era became known as the Age of Enlightenment or the Age of Reason.[28] The dominant figure in this development was the philosopher John Locke (1632–1704), whose most important writings had been published in the late seventeenth century. Following the dominant features of Newtonian mechanics, with its immutable laws governing the relationship between separate bodies, Locke developed an atomistic view of society, describing it in terms of its basic building blocks—individual (property-acquiring) human beings. Just as physicists reduced the properties of gases to the motion of their atoms, or molecules, so Locke attempted to reduce the phenomena observed in society to the behavior of discrete individual bodies.

For example, Locke justified his invention of a "natural right" to private property by claiming that the first occupation (the "taking") was less crucial than the labor (the "making") that the first taker put into the land. In making this argument, Locke pointed out—though inadvertently—that human labor, as much as land, natural resources, or animal energy, is part of nature, and that its concentration and control is no different from the concentration and control of any other resource. Indeed, exploitation is a category that can be applied both to labor and to nature, if one likes to keep them (artificially) separate.

In Locke's celebrated vision, which he saw institutionalized in the English Act of Settlement just three years before his death, state and owner are sovereigns in their respective spheres. However, the relationship between the sovereign state and the individual owner remained controversial in legal and political writings. Thomas Hobbes (1588–1679), and before him the French jurist Jean Bodin (1530–1596), in their famous theorizing about state absolutism, had given the ultimate power to the state (a view now called legal positivism). To the contrary, in the view of Locke and of the French Declaration of the Rights of Man and of the Citizen (1789), which was popular among the leading American founding fathers, ownership as a natural right, anchored in natural law, existed before the state.

DOMINATION OF THE WEST

The Peace of Westphalia (1648) finally concluded the Thirty Years' War and simplified the international legal order around a system of nation-states, fiercely independent from one another. These European states were owners of their territories, just as the ancient Roman paterfamilias had been the owner of his land. Shortly before this political compromise, ownership and sovereignty became the two organizational principles of legal modernity, structuring the individual-centered vision of law that is still with us today.

This development was boosted by the need to justify the colonization of the New World. The enterprise required that the medieval holistic vision be marginalized and that the rationalist notions of sovereignty and ownership be put fully into the service of the colonial project. The concept of legal domination of "empty" land—a notion echoing Grotius's idea of the free sea—provided the strongest intellectual justification for the exploitation of the New World, which was inhabited by "savages" with no Christian god, no rationality, and no idea of property.[29]

In the New World, the Western rational legal system, freed from holistic concerns of justice and feudal tradition, developed all its extractive potential. Freed from its medieval legacy, natural law began as a system of relationships among sovereign states and then progressively developed into a system of relationships among sovereign *individuals*. The generative, communal, life-giving attributes of property were overlooked in favor of extraction and accumulation. Individuals (both physical and legal), the atoms of the rational legal and political system, could exercise their free sovereignty not only on their own bodies but, most importantly, on private property, which was seen as a direct extension of themselves.[30] If this sovereignty had any legal limit, it could derive only from the presence of other subjects who formally had equal rights. This, of course, was not the case for non-Western political communities or for native people, who shared commons and did not formally own property. Thus, in only a few decades, the issue of whether the conquest of the Americas was legitimate had been settled, and such discussion was discontinued.

Although the sixteenth century had seen a deep scholarly debate among Spanish jurists about the legitimacy of the conquest of South America, no similar debate took place a century later during the colonization of North America.[31] By that time, the ideas of Locke and of northern European legal rationalism had already had their defining impact on the Western common thought. Among those ideas was the assertion of the fundamental right of the human mind and of science to dominate both nature and humans still in the "natural state." Both the exploitation of land and slavery—ownership of people whose human subjectivity was denied—had found a rational justification.

THE ELIMINATION OF DISTRIBUTIVE JUSTICE

By the late seventeenth century, European intellectuals, including lawyers, shared a core of fundamentally similar rationalist values. However, the medieval value system turned out to be much more resilient in legal practice, where continuity is usually stronger than change. Customary law, particularly when applied to land use in still primitive technological conditions, was scarcely compatible with any abstract, rationalist vision of the legal order. Indeed, Continental notaries and English legal practitioners were busy attempting to rationalize and recategorize the traditional medieval legal relationships that persisted as ancient feudal practices and power structures that reflected the everyday behavior of peasants, merchants, and feudal landlords.

These living practices of labor in the fields, lively city markets, or struggles among siblings to control as much as possible of their hereditary assets were difficult for any absolute lawgiver to rationalize. Medieval holism and organicism were alive and well in the countryside, in the alliances of individuals in guilds and corporations, and in the flesh and blood of the living legal system.[32]

Nonetheless, at the high table of legal reflection, there was no interest in finding the fundamental governing principles behind such practices. Lawyers could not help but participate in the humanist, rationalist vision. The issue of fair distribution *could* have been one of the foundations of legal science and private law, had it not been eclipsed by the "scientific," individual-centered vision initiated by the humanists and legally formalized by rationalist natural law in the interest of free extraction.

In the dominant Western legal ideology, never abandoned after the Peace of Westphalia, distributive justice, concerned with the whole, is constantly presented as a pre-legal idea, something located in the domain of politics or of morals. Thus, whereas commutative justice, concerned with the individual, has maintained some importance as a foundation of modern Western law (especially as a justification of contractual freedom), distributive justice was completely eliminated from the domain of legal science and has been abandoned for more than three hundred years. During this time, a rationalized version of individual-centered natural law has dominated Western legal and political thought. Absolute property rights, immune from possible redistributive plans and from any concern about the commons, represent the basis of legal support for our current disastrous model of development.

CHAPTER 4

The Great Transformation and the Legacy of Modernity

The brilliant success of Newtonian mechanics and the great prestige of Descartes's mechanistic worldview led to the gradual emergence of a rational, scientific frame of mind that eventually spread from science, through law, and into the new discipline of economics. This view embodied a critique of the communal life of most individuals—both the urban dwellers, with their guilds and corporations, and the peasants, who lived in village communities. Once bound by *duties toward one another, their communities, and their shared environment, people now were defined by their individual property rights*. Today, the legacy of the move toward modernity includes an unexamined faith in the concept of individual human rights and in a mechanistic, top-down rule of law, which opened the way for plunder and colonialism and a conception of corporations as "legal persons," themselves the building blocks of an atomized system.

The 1701 Act of Settlement in England gave birth to the modern idea of the rule of law while also excluding the commons and the political forces that represented them. The Act also illustrated a conflict between medieval and modern conceptions of law and order. Capitalism, aimed at manufacturing, had its origins in privatization, colonization, and plunder. English history shows a systematic attempt to plunder resources in faraway countries, a process that began with the Crusades even before the enclosure movement originated at home. In other words, the taking (to use Locke's term) has always had both a local and a colonial component.[1]

In England, despite occasional and sometimes violent tensions between them, the monarchy and its barons were nevertheless part of the same extractive political and institutional system.[2] Such equilibrium foreshadows the fundamental institutional setting of our present-day economic, legal, and political globalization: an alliance between those who control large amounts of property and those with political authority, ideologically hidden in a clear-cut, zero-sum distinction between the public and the private, with no space left for the commons. The social visions and structures developed between the late fifteenth and late eighteenth centuries are still largely responsible for our incapacity to put sustainable solutions to our global crisis into effect.

THE TOP-DOWN VISION OF THE LEGAL ORDER

A fundamental legacy of early modernity is the top-down vision of human law. Here the break with the medieval pluralistic vision could not be clearer. As we have seen, Roman law originally developed from the bottom up, through a process of professional conflict resolution, before Justinian consolidated and enacted it from the top down. However, Roman law did not apply equally to everyone within the boundaries of the empire. Different tribes, guilds, and ethnic or professional groups were allowed keep their own laws. Likewise, in medieval times, mercantile law was applied to merchants, Islamic law to Muslims, Jewish law to Jews, "manorial laws" in different manors, canon law to ecclesiastical matters, and so on.

In this system, known today as "legal pluralism," each social group internalized its laws, much as it maintained its own language or dialect. None of these legal systems, coexisting in the same territory, could claim final authority, nor were the different jurisdictional conflicts among them governed in any coherent way; resolutions were mainly guided by highly variable power relationships.

The idea of a single legal order, valid within jurisdictional borders, is the mature product of modernity and its legal rationalism. Human law, in this conception, is a mechanical chain of transmission of orders from the top to the bottom, to which obedience is due as a matter of respect for legality. Even the foundational conflict between natural law (in its divine or rational might) and law by design (in its political and mundane claim of authority) was ultimately to be resolved within a hierarchical order. Law by design, endowed with sovereign authority, was assumed to obey natural law and to translate it into a political order. At various times, especially during the Reformation, lesser magistrates or other political bodies were considered to have a right or even a duty to exercise resistance. It was mandatory that lesser magistrates exercise this right as a matter of duty to their constituencies. This right of resistance meant resisting law by design that was contrary to natural law, which included resisting oppression. This right or duty was never actually extended to individuals, who were always bound to obey hierarchically organized legal authorities.[3] Hierarchy was presumed to accord with natural law, unless it was challenged through the exercise of the official right of resistance. Enforcement of this hierarchy varied from place to place, but over time, the top-down legal order became the only legitimate one within each sovereign state.

In the United States, for example, the landmark *Marbury v. Madison* decision (1803) vested in the Supreme Court the fundamental power to determine the law of the land. This case established the hierarchy of sources of law, beginning at the top with the Constitution, which was based on the rationalist natural-law ideology. Any lesser law that was deemed contrary to a superior one was considered void of authority and was not to be applied by a judge.

Once power was centralized in the state and in the hierarchy of courts of law, suing became the only "right of resistance" available to individuals. Yet such action remains filtered by legal professionals in care of the machinery of the law. Direct access to making law, such as the occupation of an empty building to secure the universal right of a shelter to the homeless, or any vision of law different from this mechanistic, professionalized, hierarchical legal order has been rendered "illegal" once and for all. The consequence of disobeying the police authority tasked with the protection of private property and public spaces is immediate arrest.

For example, the lasting influence of the hierarchical vision of the legal order is experienced daily by protesters worldwide, such as those of the Occupy movement in the United States or in Hong Kong. Whoever resists state authority is deemed an enemy, not a citizen, even when the struggle is for a legitimate order of political or economic democracy. The problem of police militarization in America is one consequence of the mechanistic, top-down vision of the rule of law.

PLUNDER ABROAD

The Scientific Revolution and the subsequent successful applications of Newtonian mechanics did not happen in an economic vacuum. Tremendous economic resources were needed to establish the centralized institutional settings that would usher in what economic historian Karl Polanyi (1886–1964) called the "great transformation" at the dawn of modernity. The "primitive" accumulation of capital, necessary for the jump-start of any early capitalist social organization, was generated not only by enclosures and the transformation of the biological time of communal life into the quantifiable, alienated time of factory work, but also by seeking resources from abroad.[4]

The early political territorial powers required almost unlimited capital to complete the centralization of state authority. The fifteenth- and sixteenth-century adventures of Christopher Columbus (1451–1506), Francisco Pizarro (1475–1541), and Hernando Cortés (1485–1547) in Latin America were motivated in large part by the Castilian sovereigns' need to find the gold necessary to pay debts contracted with private bankers in Genoa and Switzerland. The legal constructions of modernity played a large role in these colonial extractions, which were carried out by denying legal dignity to previous (commons-based) legal institutions. Once again, the story involves the doctrine of private property and public sovereignty, and jurists who mixed together two legal categories that were clearly separated in Roman times.

As we have seen, classical Roman law maintained a sharp distinction between things belonging to everyone (*res communis om-*

nium) and things belonging to no one (*res nullius*). On the one hand, law, through the services of a magistrate or through "popular action," protected things of common property, such as an urban square, the high seas, or the water in the rivers and aqueducts. No individual appropriation or exclusion from access was possible. On the other hand, wild animals, fish, or forest products, which belonged to no one, could be acquired by occupation—that is, by first possession.

Taking advantage of the usual contradictions in the Roman sources, scholars in the natural-law tradition all but canceled this distinction. They made the assumption that all things—especially lands—that were not already deemed private property could be occupied, although Hugo Grotius excluded the high seas. Simple occupation seemed like a somewhat feeble legal title, however, and so natural-law scholars looked for some theory to support this assumption. For example, Grotius and Samuel Pufendorf assumed an implied consensus of the original community, a sort of tacit assent by everyone who had not previously occupied the common. In this vein, John Locke famously introduced his labor theory of property, arguing that when a person exerts labor on natural resources, those resources become that person's property. David Hume (1711–1776) used a sort of "You scratch my back, I scratch yours" argument: people recognize the good title of an occupier because they could then occupy something as well.

The idea that land not privately owned belonged to no one rather than to everyone was quickly established in order to justify the taking of land, slaves, and resources. As a consequence of this legal structure, described and justified as natural law, cargo boats could start from England full of manufactured goods (usually utensils and clothing); travel to the coast of West Africa, where these goods were traded for local sovereigns' permission to hunt slaves; leave Africa full of human property to be sold in the Americas; and come back to English ports filled with copper, tobacco, gold, tea, or guano.[5] A similar pattern, as is well known, was also happening in the direction of the East Indies, with the direct or indirect involvement of sovereign state powers.

Rationalist natural law was thus instrumental in constructing the conditions for plunder. The early acts of incorporation, which created a legal personhood as a rational expansion of physical personhood, gave corporations limited liability and the right to bear arms in order to guarantee their own survival, as theorized by Grotius in *Mare Liberum*. This legal artifact led to tremendous colonial expansion and exploitation; Roman law, rationalized by the natural-law school, provided the language and the rituals to justify the take. For instance, a notary traveled with Columbus to witness that American land, not held in private property, was *res nullius* and could therefore be occupied and owned by the Spanish Crown. The gold and silver coming from New World mines that were, at that time, unexploited was *res nullius*, and miners could acquire ownership as a matter of natural law.

Thus, the Scientific Revolution and its discovery of universal "laws of nature" bequeathed more than spectacular technological progress in weapons, maritime engineering, and cartography. It also cast in stone similarly universal human "natural laws" that have become the common understanding of modernity. The fundamental vision—given tremendous prestige by writers such as Niccolò Machiavelli (1469–1527), Jean Bodin, and Thomas Hobbes, and supported by the theology of Martin Luther (1483–1546)—was that, in secular matters of sovereignty, might makes right. Moreover, the wealth of sovereign nations could be measured by the size of the market they were able to create and control.

THE MAKING OF THE UNITED STATES

The modern vision of a rational society organized from scratch in an "empty" land was realized in the United States, based on the twin concepts of private property, vested in individuals and corporations, and sovereignty, vested in the federal system.[6] The revolutionary rupture with England, the desire to build a political system that would shield individuals from religious oppression, and the large amount of legally unoccupied land toward the west all provided ideal conditions for putting a rational legal system into practice.[7]

It is no coincidence that the most important intellectual influences among the American founding fathers were the philosophers John Locke and David Hume, the jurist William Blackstone, the economist Adam Smith (1723–1790), and the French Enlightenment philosophers, especially Voltaire (1694–1778). All these towering figures were deeply engaged in the modernist project. Blackstone in particular transferred Grotius's rationalism into the common-law tradition, while Voltaire relentlessly pursued the idea that the only way to obtain "good laws" is to discard all those of the past and make new ones. Two fundamental objectives were synthesized from that literature: a strong and effective government with concentrated executive and military authority, and a robust system of property rights. Property rights were seen as both the guardian of all other rights and an indispensable vehicle to realize the pursuit of happiness in a capitalist system. These two objectives were likely to generate some structural tension and hence were kept in harmony through a system of checks and balances, which included a complex federal system and the final word of a Supreme Court.

In the United States, the ideals of individual rights and freedom from government oppression generated a real cult of the rule of law, which was greatly amplified in this new context. Courts of law from the early nineteenth century on became the fundamental actors for dealing with human laws. Individual rights, enshrined for the first time in a constitutional bill of rights, marked the apogee of the rationalist natural-law ideal of a society made of the sum of individual component parts.

The relationship between private property and public sovereignty was frozen in the legal protection of property against government appropriation, which was allowed only in the strictest circumstances of public interest, determined by general law, and after "just compensation," defined as market value.[8] Government, on the contrary, was assumed to represent the common interest according to modern ideas of sovereignty. Thus, government could freely take from the commons and was also free to transfer the commons to private property to ensure its "development." The

Homestead Act, for instance, followed such a scheme with relation to all land outside of the thirteen earlier states.

This protection of private property and lack of any protection of commons is a mark of modernity that, perhaps more than any other, has characterized the American experience. The sovereign can privatize the commons, freely transferring common resources from the public to the private sector. Trying to do the opposite, however—transferring resources from the private sector back to the public—can be done only under strict judicial scrutiny. This imbalance does not allow for a return of the commons to the public if privatization proves mistaken, except by proving public interest and paying just compensation to the private acquirers. The process thus produces a constant and practically irreversible flux of public resources into a few private hands.

THE BIRTH OF THE "POLITICAL ECONOMY" AND ITS SCIENTIFIC TRANSFORMATION

The early theorists of economic phenomena used the ancient notion of economy in the sense of managing a household—the word *economy* is derived from the Greek *oikonomia*, which means "householding." The state was considered the household of the sovereign, and thus state policies became known as "political economy," a term that remained in use until the twentieth century, when it was replaced by the modern term *economics*.

The idea that science and knowledge must be specialized is another legacy of modernity that we have never overcome. The birth of political economy as a field of study can be seen as a progressive separation of students of behavioral laws from students of laws by design. While some jurists were developing the study of a normative legal science, others—most famously Smith—were applying their interest in political and moral philosophy, history, and society toward the foundation of this specialized discipline, now known as economics.[9]

Because of the high prestige and great success of Newtonian mechanics during the two centuries following Newton, modern economic discourse began to be considered as more or less scientific on the basis of its mathematical formalization. Scholars soon abandoned the early foundation of the theory of value, which had been based on labor, and reduced their understanding of value to the simple matter of calculating the prices that would ensure market equilibrium between supply and demand. Modern economic analysis thus takes the individual as its elementary object. In a clear move from the whole to the parts, mainstream scholars in the nineteenth and twentieth centuries abandoned the classical analysis of social classes, which had been defined in terms of historically determined relations, replacing it with analyses of the production process and surplus distribution.[10]

While this development took different political forms from country to country, in all cases centralized state authority became progressively stronger and, at the same time, was increasingly controlled by internal and international economic elites. The modern system of international law was established based on a number of equally sovereign states—"owners" of their territory—that deal with one another by means of war or, more typically, trade agreements.

The internal organization of the "household" of a sovereign nation-state determined the well-being and the wealth of the citizens. Thus, it was natural to understand the sovereign (whether a monarch or a complex political hierarchy) as the owner of public assets, and the laws governing the public and private economic activities of each nation as being in competition with each other. Within this context, the aim of the capitalist mode of production was not the satisfaction of human needs but the generation of profit and the accumulation of capital for the purpose of self-reproduction. This accumulation of national wealth became the subject of political economy, the new behavioral science that claimed autonomy from jurisprudence, philosophy, and history.

Economic historians consider William Petty's (1623–1687) *Political Arithmetick* (1690) to be the foundational work of classical political economy. Petty's thought owes much to Newton, Descartes, and Galileo. His method consisted of replacing words and arguments with numbers, weights, and measures and using rational arguments to explain economic phenomena in terms of visible natural causes. Almost one hundred years later, Adam Smith, a professor of jurisprudence and moral philosophy, well read in natural law, published *An Inquiry into the Nature and Causes of the Wealth of Nations* (1776), the first full-scale treatise on economics, written at a time when the Industrial Revolution had begun to change the face of Britain. Its importance as the foundation of modern economic theory can be compared to that of Newton's *Principia* in physics and of Charles Darwin's *On the Origin of Species* in biology.

From the prevailing Newtonian idea of the "laws of nature," which by then was perfectly coherent with the rationalist natural law, Smith deduced that it was "human nature" to barter and exchange, and he thought it natural that workers would gradually facilitate their work and improve their productivity with the help of labor-saving machinery. Smith based his economic theory on the Newtonian notions of equilibrium and laws of motion, which he immortalized in the metaphor of the "invisible hand." According to Smith, the invisible hand of the market would guide the individual self-interest of all entrepreneurs, producers, and consumers for the harmonious betterment of all—such betterment being equated with the production of material wealth. Prices would be determined in "free" markets, themselves following laws of nature such as the balancing effects of supply and demand. In this way a social result would be achieved that was independent of individual intentions, and thus an objective science of economic activity was made possible.

This idealistic picture underlies the "competitive model" widely used by economists today. Its basic assumptions include perfect and free information for all participants in a market transaction; the complete and instant mobility of displaced workers, natural resources, and machinery; and the belief that each buyer and seller in a market is small and has no influence on price. This last assumption is especially important in our discussion: the price system, like the legal system, is "out there"—being something in the nature of Descartes's *res extensa* (objective world).

Smith also thought that the self-balancing market system was one of slow and steady growth, with continually increasing demands for goods and labor. All of these conditions could never exist in practice, as Karl Marx (1818–1883) famously showed in *Capital*, yet most economists continue to use them as the basis of their theories. For example, today's politicians and economists are obsessed with the idea of unlimited economic growth, even though the absurdity of such an enterprise on a finite planet should now be obvious to all.

At the beginning of the nineteenth century, economists began to systematize their discipline in the continuing attempt to cast it into the form of a science. The first and most influential among these systematic economic thinkers was David Ricardo (1772–1823), who introduced the concept of an "economic model," a logical system of postulates and laws with a limited number of variables that could be used to describe and predict economic phenomena. The systematic efforts of Ricardo and other classical economists consolidated economics into a set of dogmas that supported the existing class structure and countered all attempts at social improvement with the "scientific" argument that the "laws of nature" (such as Ricardo's "iron law of wages," according to which the high reproduction rate of workers allows wages to be kept at a minimal level) were operating, and that the poor were responsible for their own misfortune.

In the subsequent evolution of economic thought, mainstream economics (as well as the associated legal framework) remained deeply rooted in the Cartesian-Newtonian paradigm, and today the approach of contemporary economics is fragmentary and reductionist. Economists generally fail to recognize that the economy is merely one aspect of a whole ecological and social fabric. Instead, they treat all goods equally, without considering the many ways in which these goods are related to the rest of the world, to the conditions of production, and to class composition. All values are reduced to the single criterion of increasing the size of the pie (wealth maximization).

Unfortunately, the individualistic approach of contemporary

economists, their preference for abstract quantitative models, and their inability to see economic activities within their proper ecological context have resulted in a tremendous gap between economic theory and economic reality. As a consequence, economics today is in a state of profound conceptual crisis, which became strikingly apparent during the global financial crisis originating in 2008.

In the wake of that crisis, two economics professors, Kamran Mofid and Steve Szeghi, wrote a very sober reflective essay, titled "Economics in Crisis: What Do We Tell the Students?" They argued that the standard economic theory being taught at our major universities not only may be responsible for the striking failure to predict the timing and magnitude of the events that unfolded in 2008 but also may even have been responsible for the crisis itself. Their analysis led the authors to a stark conclusion: "Now is the time to acknowledge the failures of standard theory and the narrowness of market fundamentalism. The times demand a revolution in economic thought, as well as new ways of teaching economics. In many respects this means a return to the soil in which economics was initially born, moral philosophy amid issues and questions of broad significance involving the fullness of human existence."[11]

THE CENTRAL ROLE OF CORPORATIONS AS "LEGAL PERSONS"

Early modernity produced a final legacy that continues to have a tremendous impact: the birth and development of the business corporation, granted a "legal personhood" and enjoying legal rights. The Dutch East India Company is the ancestor of our present multinational corporations, which move freely across jurisdictions to do business wherever they find the best opportunities for maximizing share value. To be attracted to these risky ventures, investors—almost invariably part of or connected with the political elite—required the lure of high returns. Moreover, their personal fortunes needed to be shielded by means of the mechanism known as limited liability, which separated their personal estates from that of the corporate legal person.[12]

To be sure, corporate forms were not an invention of modernity. They actually played a great role in the medieval legal order, especially during the Italian Renaissance, when the economic and political organization of the city-states was based on corporate guilds and factions rather than on individuals. The Dutch East India Company, however, represented not only a change in the size and strength of the corporate form but also the first example of a private ownership structure that claimed legal advantages even over states, thanks to the skill of their lawyers. The legal weapon of this early transnational capitalist entity was natural law, which was deployed for the first time in a highly creative way and transformed into international law by the legal genius of Grotius, who served throughout his life as a legal advocate and well-paid consultant for the company.

According to Grotius, the sea was a common; by its nature it could not be an object of ownership but was to remain open to all. For a legal "person" doing business in international trade, access to this common was of vital importance, to the point that its defense of this access was grounded in the very fundamental natural right to exist—the natural-law foundation of every other right. A legal "person" could resist, even by violence, a violation of this right if its fundamental right of existence was endangered. With this argument, Grotius successfully defended his client's right to roam the commons, the oceans. He subsequently presented a natural-law justification of the company's right to acquire private property that was left unused, and was thus *res nullius*, even when it was found in a territory under foreign jurisdiction.

Grotius, who was in his early twenties when he made this extraordinarily smart move, enabled the theory of natural law in northern Europe to go beyond any controversy about whether indigenous people had rights or political agency. Regardless of the solution of this problem, private persons could acquire property rights on *res nullius* under any kind of jurisdiction, according to the natural law that human law by design must always respect. To Grotius and his corporate clients, this principle was especially important because of the implications for the possible extraction of untapped mineral resources.

From the beginning, the aggregate of natural rights to do business without political obligations to other governments has created a very favorable playing field for private corporations venturing into transnational activities. Very similar legal arguments were advanced by British authorities to protect the right of British companies to deal opium in China or to open markets in Latin America. And very similar arguments are today the foundation of the World Trade Organization: no public power can limit the corporate right to roam the globe to acquire control over natural or human resources.[13]

CHAPTER 5

From the Machine to the Network

Scientific Thought in the Nineteenth
and Twentieth Centuries

Despite the continued success of Newtonian mechanics throughout the eighteenth and nineteenth centuries, some people voiced a strong opposition to this mechanistic worldview. In addition, several developments in nineteenth-century science—the theory of evolution, the investigation of electric and magnetic phenomena, and thermodynamics—made the limitations of the Newtonian model apparent and prepared the way for the scientific revolutions of the twentieth century.

THE ROMANTIC MOVEMENT

Even before the limits of Newtonian mechanics became apparent to scientists, the Romantics were already questioning this purely mechanistic approach. The Romantic movement in art, literature, music, philosophy, science, and law, which arose in the late eighteenth century, stood in opposition to the mechanistic worldview of Newtonian science and Enlightenment philosophy.[1] The Romantics were not altogether opposed to the Enlightenment's emphasis on reason, but they argued that scientific reasoning should be accompanied by aesthetic judgment, which offered another, complementary path to understanding the nature of reality. The Romantics fundamentally questioned the role of mechanism as the dominant scientific paradigm; they replaced the concept of mechanism with that of "the organic" as the chief principle for interpreting nature.

William Blake (1757–1827), the mystical poet and painter who exerted a strong influence on English Romanticism, was a passionate critic of Newton. He contemptuously referred to the tendency of reducing all phenomena to underlying mechanical laws as a "single vision," epitomizing his critique in the celebrated lines, "May God us keep / From single vision and Newton's sleep."

Likewise, the German Romantics had a broad interest in philosophy, art, and science. Their dialogues moved easily from poetry to biology, aesthetics, history, and anthropology. In biology, their central focus was the nature of organic form. Johann Wolfgang von Goethe (1749–1832), the central figure of the movement, coined the term *morphology* for the study of biological form; he conceived of form as a pattern of relationships within an organized whole. The term and this conception remain at the forefront of systems thinking today.

The Romantic view of nature as "one great harmonious whole," as Goethe put it, led some scientists of that period to extend their search for wholeness to the entire planet and to see the Earth as an integrated whole, a living being. In doing so, they revived the ancient tradition that had begun with the Greek conception of the world as a *kósmos* and had flourished throughout the Middle Ages and the Renaissance, until the medieval outlook was replaced by the Cartesian image of the world as a machine. The view of the Earth as a living being, dormant for only a relatively brief period, had been revived. The views of the living Earth developed by Leonardo da Vinci in the fifteenth century and by the Romantic scientists in the eighteenth contain some key elements of our contemporary Gaia theory of a living planet.

EVOLUTIONARY THOUGHT IN THE LIFE SCIENCES

At the turn of the eighteenth to the nineteenth century, under the influence of the Romantic movement, the primary concern of biologists was the problem of biological form; questions of material composition were secondary. This emphasis was especially true for the French school of comparative anatomy, or morphology, pioneered by Georges Cuvier (1769–1832), who created a system of zoological classification based on similarities of structural relations.

One of the key insights of Romantic biology was that nature's living forms exhibit fundamental organic types, often called "archetypes," which are subject to gradual variations, a theory that Charles Darwin (1809–1882) acknowledged as playing a central role in his early conception of evolution. This new trend of thinking went beyond the image of the Newtonian world-machine and would dominate all future scientific thought.

The notion of evolution—of gradual change, growth, and development—first arose in geology, where careful studies of fossils led scientists to the idea that the present state of the Earth is the result of continuous development caused by the action of natural forces over immense periods of time. This idea formed the intellectual background for the most precise and far-reaching formulation of evolutionary thought: the theory of the evolution of species in biology, first tentatively formulated by Jean-Baptiste Lamarck (1744–1829) and a few decades later established by Darwin. Darwin's monumental *On the Origin of Species* (1859) and theory of evolution forced scientists to abandon the Cartesian conception of the world as a machine that had emerged fully constructed from the hands of its creator. Instead, the universe had to be pictured as an evolving, ever-changing system in which complex structures developed from simpler forms.[2]

EVOLUTIONARY THOUGHT IN PHYSICS

As this new way of thinking was elaborated in the life sciences, evolutionary concepts were also emerging in physics. However, while biological evolution was conceived of as being a movement toward increasing order and complexity, evolution in physics came to mean just the opposite—a movement toward increasing disorder.

The crisis in Newtonian physics was triggered by the discovery and investigation of electric and magnetic phenomena, which involved a new type of force that could not be described appropriately by the mechanistic model. Michael Faraday (1791–1867) and later James Clerk Maxwell (1831–1879) not only studied the effects of electric and magnetic forces but also made the forces themselves the primary objects of their investigation. By replacing the concept of a force with the much subtler concept of a field, they were the first to go beyond Newtonian physics, showing that fields had their own reality and could be studied without any reference to material bodies. Their theory, known as electrodynamics, culminated in the realization that light is in fact a rapidly alternating electromagnetic field traveling through space in the form of waves.

The application of Newtonian mechanics to the study of thermal phenomena led physicists to the formulation of thermodynamics, based on the recognition that heat is the energy generated by complicated motions of atoms and molecules. Thermodynamics was formulated in terms of two fundamental laws. The first is the law of conservation of energy, which states that the total energy involved in a process is always conserved. It may change its form, but none of it is lost. The second law of thermodynamics states that, while the total energy involved in a process is always constant, the amount of *useful* energy is diminishing, dissipating into heat, friction, and so on. Mechanical energy is dissipated into heat and cannot be completely recovered. In other words, physical processes proceed in a certain direction, from order to disorder; according to classical physics, the universe as a whole is moving toward ever-increasing disorder. It is running down and will eventually grind to a halt. This grim picture of cosmic evolution stood in sharp contrast to the evolutionary idea held by biologists, who observed that living nature evolves from disorder to order, toward states of ever-increasing complexity.

By the end of the nineteenth century, therefore, Newtonian mechanics had lost its role as the fundamental theory of natural phenomena, and the Newtonian image of the universe as a perfectly running machine had been supplemented by two diametrically opposed views of evolutionary change—that of a living world unfolding toward increasing order and complexity, and that of an engine running down, a world of ever-increasing disorder.

It took another century to resolve the paradox of these contradictory views of evolution. In the 1970s, Ilya Prigogine (1917–2003) realized that the second law of thermodynamics applies to isolated, or "closed," physical systems, whereas biological systems are always open to flows of energy and matter (or food). In biological evolution, overall disorder keeps increasing, but this increase is not uniform. In the living world, order and disorder are always created simultaneously. For example, when we eat a carrot, we diminish its structure, thereby increasing its disorder, but we use its components to maintain or even increase the order of our own organism. As Prigogine put it, "Living organisms are islands of order in a sea of disorder." They maintain and even increase their order at the expense of greater disorder in their environment.

THE CONCEPTUAL REVOLUTION IN PHYSICS

At the end of the nineteenth century, Maxwell's theory of electrodynamics and Darwin's theory of evolution had clearly gone beyond the Cartesian/Newtonian model and indicated that the universe is far more complex than either Descartes or Newton had imagined. The basic ideas underlying Newtonian physics, though insufficient to explain all natural phenomena, were nevertheless still believed to be correct. However, this situation changed radically during the first three decades of the twentieth century. Two new theories of physics—quantum theory and relativity theory—shattered all the principal concepts of the Cartesian worldview and of Newtonian mechanics. Notions such as absolute space and time, elementary solid particles, a fundamental material substance, the strictly causal nature of physical phenomena, or an objective description of nature could not be extended to the new domains into which twentieth-century physics penetrated.[3]

Perhaps the greatest shock was the discovery that, at the subatomic level, the world could no longer be decomposed into independent, elementary units. Ever since Newton, physicists had believed that all physical phenomena could be reduced to the properties of hard and solid material particles. But as they shifted their attention from macroscopic objects to atoms and subatomic particles, nature did not reveal any isolated building blocks. Molecules and atoms do consist of components—protons, electrons, quarks, and so forth. However, these components cannot be understood as isolated entities but must be defined through their interrelations. A subatomic particle is, in essence, a set of relationships that reach outward to other things, which are themselves sets of relationships.

In the formalism of quantum mechanics, these relationships are expressed in terms of probabilities, and the probabilities are determined by the dynamics of the whole system. Whereas in classical mechanics the properties and behavior of the parts determine those of the whole, the situation is reversed in quantum mechanics: it is the whole that determines the behavior of the parts. This conceptual shift from the parts to the whole represented a spectacular breakdown of Cartesian mechanism and of Descartes's celebrated method of analytical thinking, of analyzing complicated problems in terms of their components.

As scientists became increasingly aware of the approximate nature of the laws of Newtonian physics, they also stopped using the term "law of nature." Max Planck's (1858–1947) law of blackbody radiation (1900), which triggered the conceptual revolutions of quantum physics, is perhaps the last example of this term being used. Afterward, we had Albert Einstein's (1879–1955) mass-energy *equivalence* ($E = mc^2$), Niels Bohr's (1885–1962) *postulates* (his model of the atom), Wolfgang Pauli's (1900–1958) exclusion *principle*, and Werner Heisenberg's (1901–1976) uncertainty *principle*—none of them formulated in terms of "laws."

A critical insight with far-reaching consequences is the fact that the universal interwovenness revealed by quantum physics always includes the human observer and his or her consciousness. We can never speak about nature without, at the same time, speaking of ourselves. In the words of Heisenberg, "What we observe is not nature itself, but nature exposed to our method of questioning."[4] As the Greeks and other ancient peoples had understood, the whole is more than just an aggregate of parts. All components of the universe are interconnected, and people, in turn, are connected with the universe in a very real way.

SYSTEMS THINKING IN THE LIFE SCIENCES

While quantum physicists struggled with the conceptual shift from the parts to the whole, a similar shift was taking place in the life sciences. In the 1920s, German biologists elaborated and refined many of the key insights of the Romantic biologists of the eighteenth century. Calling their new discipline "organismic biology," they asserted that living organisms are integrated wholes that cannot be understood from the study of their parts alone.

The organismic biologists also engaged in interdisciplinary dialogues with psychologists, who discussed the process of perception in terms of integrated perceptual patterns—meaningful organized wholes, which exhibit qualities that are absent in their parts. For instance, when we meet a friend and notice that she seems to be sad, that perception of sadness is informed by a multitude of subtle facial expressions, gestures, tone of voice, and so forth, which we would not even be able to analyze but which our brain integrates into a single perceptual pattern. Psychologists borrowed the German word *Gestalt*, meaning organic form, and used it to denote those integrated perceptual patterns. Accordingly, their discipline became known as Gestalt psychology.

The third discipline contributing to these dialogues about wholeness was the new science of ecology, which had emerged from the school of "organicism" (the study of the nature of organic form) during the nineteenth century, when biologists began to study communities of organisms. While biologists encountered irreducible wholeness in organisms and psychologists found it in perception, ecologists encountered it in their studies of animal and plant communities in ecosystems. They realized that the members of ecological communities are all interlinked and form networks of relationships, such as food webs, in which the success of the whole community depends on the success of its individual members and the success of each member, in turn, depends on the success of the community as a whole.

From these interdisciplinary dialogues emerged a new way of thinking that became known as "systems" or "systemic" thinking.[5]

The common field of study was living systems, which include individual organisms, parts of organisms, and communities of organisms, such as social systems or ecosystems. Thus, living systems span a very broad range, and systems thinking is by its nature an interdisciplinary or, better still, a "transdisciplinary" approach.

Gestalt psychologist Christian von Ehrenfels (1859–1932) popularized Aristotle's contention that "the whole is greater than the sum of its parts," and this became a common slogan among systems theorists. Living systems are integrated wholes whose properties cannot be reduced to those of smaller parts. Their essential properties arise from the interactions and relationships among the parts.

The shift in focus from objects to relationships runs counter to the traditional scientific enterprise in Western culture, with its focus on things that can be measured and weighed. Relationships cannot be measured and weighed; relationships must be mapped. These shifts of emphasis—from the parts to the whole, from objects to relationships, from measuring to mapping—are all part of the tension between the study of matter (quantity) and the study of form (quality). The discussion of matter uses the language of physics and chemistry to describe material structures, forces, and their resulting processes. The discussion of form, by contrast, involves an abstract mapping of relationships to describe patterns of organization, such as networks or feedback loops.

LIVING NETWORKS

Ecologists describe ecosystems as communities of plants, animals, and microorganisms linked together in networks through feeding relations. They introduced the notion of food webs and, more generally, of the web of life. Food webs are networks of organisms, organisms are networks of cells, and cells are networks of molecules. Thus, wherever we see life, we see networks, and the network has become the key metaphor of our time, just as the machine was the key metaphor for three hundred years after Descartes and Newton. Whereas a machine is properly analyzed in terms of its parts, a network is analyzed in terms of its links or relationships. This understanding embodies the shift from mechanistic to systemic thinking.

As the network concept became increasingly prominent in ecology, systemic thinkers began to use network models at all systems levels, viewing organisms as networks of cells, organs, and organ systems, just as ecosystems are understood as networks of individual organisms. Correspondingly, the flows of matter and energy through ecosystems were perceived as the continuation of the metabolic pathways through organisms. These two aspects of living systems—networks and flows—are two key concepts of the new systemic conception of life that has emerged during the last three decades.

NONLINEAR SYSTEMS

The basic concepts of systems thinking were developed and refined during the 1920s and 1930s. The 1940s then saw the formulation of actual systems theories that integrated systems concepts into coherent frameworks that describe the principles of the organization of living systems. These classical systems theories include general systems theory, developed by the biologist Ludwig von Bertalanffy (1901–1972), and the theory of cybernetics, which was the result of a multidisciplinary collaboration between mathematicians, neuroscientists, social scientists, and engineers.

The next phase of systems thinking came in the 1970s and 1980s, with the development of new models and theories of living systems that are far superior to the classical systems theories. The distinctive feature of these new theories was a new mathematical language that enabled scientists for the first time to handle the enormous complexity of living systems mathematically. Chaos theory and fractal geometry are important branches of this new mathematics, which is popularly known as complexity theory.

The crucial characteristic of complexity theory is that it is a nonlinear mathematics. Its technical name, accordingly, is nonlinear dynamics. Until recently, scientists tended to avoid nonlinear equations because they are very difficult to solve. For example, the smooth flow of water in a river, in which there are no obstacles, is described by a linear equation. But when a rock in the river causes the water to swirl, the river becomes turbulent. The movement of water becomes so complicated that it seems quite chaotic, and this complex motion can be described by nonlinear equations.

In the 1970s, scientists for the first time had powerful high-speed computers that could help them tackle such nonlinear equations. In doing so, they devised a new kind of mathematical language that revealed very surprising patterns under the seemingly chaotic behavior of nonlinear systems—order beneath the apparent chaos. When a nonlinear equation is solved using these new techniques, the result is not a formula but a visual shape, a pattern traced by the computer. The strange attractors of chaos theory and the fractals of fractal geometry are examples of such patterns. They are visual descriptions of a system's complex dynamics. The new complexity mathematics is essentially a mathematics of patterns and relationships.

During the past thirty years, the strong interest in nonlinear phenomena has generated a series of new and powerful theories that have dramatically increased our understanding of many key characteristics of life. In particular, two systemic theories have led to major advances in understanding the two key characteristics of life mentioned above, networks and flows.

The first of these theories is a theory of living networks, known as the theory of autopoiesis, developed by Humberto Maturana and Francisco Varela.[6] According to this theory, the defining characteristic of living networks is that they are self-generating, or "autopoietic"—from the Greek *auto* (self) and *poiein* (to make). For example, all the biological structures within a cell—the proteins, enzymes, DNA, and so on—are continually produced, repaired, and regenerated by the cellular network. Likewise, bodily cells in a multicellular organism are continually regenerated and recycled by the organism's metabolic network. Living networks continually create or recreate themselves by transforming or replacing their components. In this way they undergo continual structural changes while preserving their weblike patterns of organization.

Once again we encounter the coexistence of stability and change—one of the key characteristics of life. What remains stable is the system's pattern of organization, the network; what continually changes is the organism's structure.

The other pioneering systemic theory deals with the constant flow of energy and matter through these living networks. This is Prigogine's theory of dissipative structures, which explains how living systems are able to maintain the same overall structure despite an overall flow and change of components. Prigogine coined the term "dissipative structure" to emphasize the close association, at first paradoxical, between structure and order on the one hand, and flow and change (dissipation) on the other; once again, stability and change coexist.[7]

The dynamics of dissipative structures specifically include the spontaneous emergence of new forms of order. Although living systems generally remain in a stable state, every now and then they encounter points of instability where either a breakdown occurs or, more frequently, new forms of order spontaneously emerge. This spontaneous emergence of order at critical points of instability, which is often referred to simply as "emergence," is one of the hallmarks of life. It has been recognized as the dynamic origin of development, learning, and evolution. In other words, creativity—the generation of new forms—is a key property of all living systems.

LIVING NETWORKS IN THE SOCIAL DOMAIN

A framework to extend the systemic understanding of life to the social domain, and in particular to human laws, rests on the assumption that life has a fundamental unity and that different living systems exhibit similar patterns of organization. Evolution has proceeded for billions of years by using the same patterns again and again. As life evolves, these patterns tend to become more and more elaborate, but they are always variations on the same basic themes. The network pattern, in particular, is one of the very basic patterns of organization in all living systems. At all levels, the components and processes of living systems are interlinked in networks. Extending the systemic conception of life to the social domain, therefore, means applying our knowledge of life's basic patterns and principles of organization, and specifically our understanding of living networks, to social reality.[8]

Social networks are networks of communications. In the human realm, this means that we need to consider our whole inner world of consciousness and culture—of ideas, values, goals, conflicts, relationships of power, and so on—to properly understand these communications. Like biological networks, social networks are self-generating, but what they generate is mostly nonmaterial. Each communication creates thoughts and meaning, which give rise to further communications, and thus the entire network generates itself. As communications continue in a social network, they form multiple feedback loops that eventually produce a shared system of beliefs, explanations, and values, also known as culture, which is continually sustained by further communications. Through this culture, individuals acquire identities as members of the social network, and in this way the network generates its own boundary.

CHAPTER 6

Mechanical Jurisprudence

O nce more, legal developments following the triumph of Cartesian legal rationalism show remarkable parallels with developments in the natural sciences. Evolutionary thought and Romanticism had discredited the mechanistic vision of natural law as an immutable universal system of rational rules rooted in human reason. Nevertheless, the evolutionary and Romantic critique was unsuccessful in displacing the mechanistic vision of law from its mainstream status and disrupting its influence over the current vision and practice of Western professionalized law.

The resilience of the mechanistic approach in human laws is due to its invaluable service to the needs of nineteenth-century capitalism. The reduction of the legal system to an agreement between private property and state sovereignty has been a powerful tool in quashing nature and community. The dominant conception of law is still that of an objective, state-governed system with the power to decide conflicts between value-extracting subjects. No alternative community-based understanding of law has ever reemerged. To the contrary, somewhat paradoxically, the evolution of legal theory has transformed both Romantic and evolutionary challenges to the mechanistic vision into an ideological component of the dominant capitalist extractive model. The outcome of this process is the current global brand of legal positivism that locks us into understanding law as an unchallengeable technology that we can access, if at all, only through professionals. A systemic vision of the nature of law as a living network of communities allowing for the "emergence" of new legal forms in order to sustain the survival of our planet is still to come. Even so, a number of ideas developed by Romantic and evolutionary thinking are relevant for our ecology of law (which we have previously defined as a legal order that is consistent with and honors the basic principles of ecology).

THE FRENCH NAPOLEONIC CODE AND MECHANICAL JURISPRUDENCE

In the legal domain, the Cartesian worldview reached dominant status in France with the triumph of the French Revolution. The rationalization of the French legal system, elaborated by Jean Domat, roughly corresponds to the work of William Blackstone in England almost one hundred years later. Both were attempts to place existing, highly disordered legal materials into a coherent, rational form. Napoleon's French Civil Code of 1804 borrowed doctrines and ideas from Domat.

As with other Continental legal philosophies, private property and state sovereignty are the fundamental building blocks of the Napoleonic Code. This hierarchical vision of the legal order, in which the sovereign state and the sovereign owner are in direct consensual relationship with each other, is "legal absolutism."[1] A number of fundamental legal doctrines of the Code are classic, individualistic Cartesian ideas, coherent with the need to transform commons into capital. Among these ideas, we find the Code's emphatic definition of ownership as the right to enjoy and dispose of a thing in the most absolute way; the idea of the contractual agreement binding the parties as law; the notion of transfer of ownership by pure consent; the fault principle in tort liability, which shields entrepreneurs from legal responsibility for damages produced without fault while doing business; and the coexistence of natural and legal personhood, which shields the personal fortune of corporate investors by making the corporation liable instead of them. Through these and other technical devices, Napoleon incorporated the Cartesian vision into the Code. For instance, Article 5 of the Code limits judges to the mechanical application of the

Code to the facts of the situation in front of them, a vision that Dean Roscoe Pound (1870–1964) of Harvard Law School called "mechanical jurisprudence."[2] The Code, conceived of as written reason, was supposed to be applied with very little, if any, interpretation, purely through Cartesian logic applied by a branch of the state, the judiciary.

Through military conquest or intellectual reputation, the Code became the backbone of professionalized law across the world.[3] The tremendous success of rationalism, together with the political resistance against Napoleonic modernization, triggered the Romantic reaction, especially in Germany.

EVOLUTION IN LEGAL THOUGHT

We have seen how, under the influence of the Romantic movement, both evolutionary and holistic thinking became highly developed in philosophy and science. In jurisprudence, an idea of legal evolution gained currency in the late eighteenth century, especially within Scottish legal and philosophical circles.[4] David Hume described three fundamental laws stemming from the very fact of groups of people living together: "stability of possession, its transferability by consent, and the performance of promises." These arrangements do not stem from reason, Hume maintained, but from a general sense of common interest in which people gradually become conscious of the need to regulate their conduct according to rules. Every rule, like language or the recognition of gold as a medium of exchange, "arises gradually and acquires force by a slow progression, and by our repeated experience of the inconveniences of transgressing it."[5]

Charles-Louis Montesquieu (1689–1755), one of the great political philosophers of the Enlightenment, was the recognized pioneer of a scientific idea of evolution in the law, which implied a development of society from one stage to the next. This conception is still deployed today in many writings on "underdevelopment," authored by scholars known as development economists (who study economic processes in low-income countries). Montesquieu compared a variety of societies to determine which aspects of law could be found everywhere, no matter how different such societies were in climate, customs, geography, or stage of development. By this method, he could determine scientifically the foundational nature of private property for the most advanced societies.

While in science, evolutionary thinking was striking a hard blow to the Cartesian mechanistic vision, in law it was reinforcing its conclusions by giving scientific strength to the kind of possessive individualism that capitalist development needed. Lawyers provided the pincers of private property and state sovereignty with the legitimating vision of legal evolution as a four-stage process of development, based on social means of subsistence. A society would theoretically develop gradually from a hunter-gatherer society (stage 1); to a nomadic society based on pastoralism and cattle breeding (stage 2); to a society based on agriculture (stage 3); and, finally, to a society based on commerce (stage 4). This linear idea is still dominant in economic thinking. On the one hand, as Darwin's theory had done in science, this theory provided an early critique to the idea of abstract universal rational natural law, but, on the other hand, it confirmed its individualistic vision. Through these stages, legal institutions, particularly government and most notably property, evolved from simple arrangements to structures of ever-increasing complexity.[6]

LEGAL ROMANTICISM

Montesquieu's scientific paradigm, rather than discrediting the mechanistic vision of law, ended up reinforcing its conclusions. Likewise, the German Romantic jurist and historian Friedrich Karl von Savigny (1779–1861) criticized the abstract concept of a universal legal order but eventually reinforced its most relevant legal conclusions. Savigny, the nineteenth century's most influential jurist, was a conservative, perhaps reactionary aristocrat who feared the enactment of the Napoleonic Code, which he considered an unsophisticated legal document, lacking sufficient academic elaboration. Savigny based his critique on two ideas. First, because the law varies from place to place, it cannot be seen as an abstract mathematical order of the Newtonian type. Instead, because it reflects different national characters and ambitions, it must be the product of the "spirit of the people" (*Volksgeist*), making every society discrete, as interpreted by its intellectuals and jurists. It is clear that Savigny was using a notion of historical transformation with a strong evolutionary flavor as his fundamental critique of rationalist natural law. The Cartesian Napoleonic Code, he argued, did not reflect any other spirit than that of the French, who through their Revolution had made it their law.

Second, Savigny argued that the law belonged not to the sovereign state but, like culture or language, to the people, who could express it through the work of their academic jurists. Law must respect the spirit of each place and of each historical time. Any codification of law was a top-down act of authority of the state in a given historical moment that necessarily made law less adaptable to subsequent historical circumstances. Because of this insight, famously expressed during a polemic about codification with Anton Friedrich Justus Thibaut (1772–1840), Savigny's Romanticism is also known as legal historicism. While the methodological contributions of Savigny are sound, potentially giving back some life to the law, the Romantic critique of mechanism in law proved practically ineffective as German legal Romantics divided into two fiercely opposing camps.

The strict followers of Savigny believed, somewhat paradoxically, that the Roman law displayed the real spirit of German people because Roman law was still applied law in the courts.[7] On the other hand, the "Germanists" felt that the spirit of German folk law in its customary form competed with Roman law after the fall of the empire. This law was communal, based not on a system of individualistic, formalized property rights but rather on a much more flexible system of tenure adaptable to the necessities of close-knit communities.[8]

The wealth of Germanic elaboration shows that because of the pervasive alliance between capital and law, which serves unrestrained individual property, "community" has not developed into a legal notion capable of reflecting the values of our time. While Savigny's notion of the "empire of individual will" has triumphed as an even broader justification of unrestrained property rights, it might have been possible that the traditionally closed community, in the hands of jurists capable of reflecting changing social conditions, could have progressively opened up to serve the needs of an ecological legal order. However, in spite of this theoretical possibility, dominant legal Romanticism did not disturb but rather emphasized the fundamental Roman law–based, individualistic idea of Western law.

THE PROFESSIONALIZATION OF LAW

The legacy of legal Romanticism, far from being a desirable injection of living culture and collective political agency into the law, was a further step in the professionalization of law. In the twentieth and twenty-first centuries, the transmission of legal knowledge from one generation to the next has become exclusively a matter of academic legal profesionalization. This process has entirely marginalized any bottom-up, community-produced legal custom, and it has completely insulated law from its own ecology. The only choice available in law today remains that between the interests of private property and state sovereignty—a formidable legal constraint that precludes us from imagining any alternative vision. The only legitimate political choice in Western society is between more or less government and more or less property. The law has progressively become a technology to support this constriction of political agency.

Despite the promises of Savigny's Romantic thought, German legal academia generated a jurisprudence of concepts even more abstract than their natural-law counterparts. German jurists developed what legal philosopher Duncan Kennedy has called "classic legal consciousness": a methodology of formalistic, highly professionalized, deductive legal learning, based on the unrestrained freedom of individual will that spread throughout the world.[9] After Germany itself codified private law in 1900, jurists worldwide agreed that law in advanced societies was a pure system, ontologically separate and different from politics, morality, justice, religion, or cultural norms. This formalistic legal positivism, which maintains that law has a purely objective framework and is a system in the domain of facts and not of values (which are left to the political process), became the only canon of Western law.

In the United States, professional legal education became rooted in academic institutions. The founding dean of Harvard Law School, Christopher Columbus Langdell (1826–1906), said that the lawyer was like a biologist, and that cases as contained in law reports were laboratory materials, from which general doctrines could be induced to apply to other cases. Langdell's method, known as legal formalism, together with his "Socratic method" of academic legal instruction, spread through the United States, producing entire generations of lawyers alienated from any ecological understanding of their subject matter.[10] No context, historical or social, let alone political, is ever given in academic instruction of the law (except sometimes in marginal, optional curricular offerings of a few hours in comparative law, sociology of law, or legal history). Students read their cases and discuss them in the abstract, developing an initiated jargon and technical skills for interpreting cases and statutes—skills that have been fundamentally the same since the early origins of Roman law.

This process of professionalization has taken law away from communities, expropriating this most fundamental "common"— a community's control over its own legal order. When laws are determined far away, communities are disempowered and individuals have little incentive to bond in order to change the world where they live. Although this expropriation has occasionally produced desirable results when close communities show excluding attitudes—such as in the formal desegregation of the American South—it more often is lethal for the environment and for community identity itself. For instance, land development decisions follow the logic of a choice between private property and government interests. Academic lawyers portray these two as conflicting interests, but, in fact, both obey the very same logic of value extraction. Likewise, issues such as access to justice, tort reform, availability of punitive damages—all of which tremendously impact the well-being of communities—are decided by lawyers in different capacities at levels completely remote from the communities themselves.[11]

The substance of this choice did not change even when the next dominant American movement, "legal realism" (which offered a description of law in action rather than in books), questioned legal formalism very harshly in the aftermath of World War I, in order to tackle the challenges produced by so-called socialist legality in the USSR. Massive urbanization, industrial production, war efforts, and interwar crises created new problems for which the legal answer—more government and less private property—remained entirely within the limits set by the opposition between private law (market) and public law (state) in both the capitalist and the Soviet blocs. This opposition increased the alienation of law from community and in the United States led to more legal professionalization of the political process of law making. Law professors from elite law schools staffed federal agencies in the United States. Thus, beginning with the New Deal, technical legal reasoning merged with actual political power, producing a distinct form of technocracy. Progressive political choices, rather than being described as such, were hidden behind the technical expertise of lawyers, just as today conservative political choices are hidden behind the expertise of economists pursuing the growth of the gross domestic product or the flexibility of the labor market.

Legal realism caused a particular form of merger between lawyers and social scientists within elite American schools,[12] an encounter that set the premises for what is known as the economic analysis of law, which has become the dominant form of worldwide legal consciousness in the aftermath of the collapse of the Soviet Union. The realist idea that legal analysis is a "social science" rather than a "natural science" made it subservient to economics, the recognized queen of social sciences. Under the influence of mainstream economists, the dominant vision of law shared by legal professionals gradually evolved from an aggregate of positive

scientific concepts from which to deduce rules into a kind of social engineering, a means to the end, for market efficiency. In this
vision, the political process produces law by design and reflects
the struggle of competing interest groups. Once a law is passed,
the lawyers, and only the lawyers, adapt it to the requirements
of the legal system and interpret it in the context of making a
market-friendly society. This process professionally insulates legal
principles and rules from the mutable political preferences and
desires that carry inefficiency in the system.[13] In this vision, there
is no space for the community to give meaning to law, nor for significant local variations. Thus, the dominant jurisprudential view
reinvigorates the myth of the scientific predictability of law as a
prerequisite for the efficient arrangement of business activity. Because the same fundamental laws of the market govern economics, whether in Bombay, New York, or Brazzaville, investors everywhere must encounter equivalent market-friendly legal systems.
This dominant conception transforms the law from (local) culture
to (global) technology.

CHAPTER 7

The Mechanistic Trap

D espite the shift of metaphors from the machine to the network at the forefront of science, the mechanistic worldview of modernity still holds sway among lawyers, political leaders, and executives. Only during the past two decades, for instance, have organizational theorists begun to apply systems thinking to the management of human institutions. The mechanistic view of organizations also remains widespread among managers, who act within institutional constraints created by law, which has itself been transformed into a technology and no longer specifically reflecting the will of a community. This view creates a kind of mechanistic trap in which human agents are no longer able to control the actions of legal institutions such as corporations or government bureaucracies, even when such actions are detrimental to communities or the environmental commons.

SHORTSIGHTED INCENTIVE SCHEMES

The narrow pursuit of the bottom line finds a key of success in the legal technique of outsourcing. The dominant legal vision makes it all but an imperative to outsource manufacturing from advanced industrial countries to countries where workers and the environment are exploited beyond any reason. For example, in April 2013, the collapse of the Rana Plaza building in Bangladesh killed more than 1,100 poor workers, who had been threatened with being fired and who were forced into factories to fulfill contractual obligations toward the most famous Western brands, from Gap to Benetton.[1] Because of the legal structure of outsourcing, corporations making huge profits on the exploitation of labor formally employed by different companies are shielded from responsibility for such tragedies. Their CEOs thus routinely deploy such legal techniques. CEOs and boards of directors are located far from where their decisions will have dramatic impact, and corporate charters make such decisions almost obligatory. Even the most humane CEO or legal counsel, because of legally distorted feedback loops, will feel bound by his or her legal obligations toward shareholders to pursue ecologically and socially devastating business opportunities that promise immediate returns.

Such decision-making structures are dramatically shortsighted from the social and ecological point of view. For example, at the very beginning of this century, in pursuit of tax benefits and cheap land for building a new corporate headquarters, Pfizer negotiated with local authorities to relocate to the impoverished city of New London, Connecticut. The deal required a controversial change in the established law of eminent domain in favor of the pharmaceutical giant at the expense of local small property owners and generated tremendous social costs. The issue went all the way to the Supreme Court. In the controversial 2005 *Kelo v. City of New London* decision, the Supreme Court considered the promise of new jobs and taxes offered by Pfizer sufficient to establish the public interest in eminent domain. Just a few years after this highly controversial decision, however, Pfizer decided to close the new headquarters, firing 1,400 employees and leaving behind empty buildings and social ruin. Forty states passed anti-Kelo laws to limit the impact of the business-friendly Supreme Court.

Worldwide, there are many such examples of corporations relentlessly pursuing shareholder interest, working as legally determined machines, and externalizing social costs. Corporate behavior is thus as much a cultural as a legal problem. The transformation of corporate charters to force management to take the real costs of their actions into consideration by deploying systemic thought is one of the crucial steps necessary to accomplish an ecology of law.[2]

Similar legally induced institutional constraints and incentives tend to determine the behavior of professional politicians, who operate within the short time span of the election cycle. Even if a politician has a genuinely ecological and systemic vision, the results of any corresponding policy he or she could enact would be visible only in the medium to long term. However, the extra costs perceived by their constituencies (and especially by their financial donors) would be felt immediately in the form of environmental and social obligations, a requirement to upgrade technologies, and so forth. This discrepancy between short election cycles and long-term results explains the lukewarm help that politicians tend to offer to environmental movements. The fear of losing elections by alienating the oil industry, for example, explains why the environmental movement is left alone in every struggle against pipelines, and why West Virginia legislators do not confront the coal industry. Well-known U.S. politicians such as Democrat Jim Jontz (1951–2007) and Republican Wayne Gilchrest had their political careers cut short when corporate money flooded to their opponents in retaliation for their environmental stances. A school of thought known as "rational choice theory," popular among lawyers, economists, and political scientists, has theorized that it is "irrational" for politicians not to maximize their chances of being re-elected. A Nobel Prize was even awarded to economist James Buchanan for his work on this theory.[3] A conscientious politician standing for the environment or for the rights of the powerless is therefore seen as irrational in today's dominant academic wisdom. Thus, in order for representative politics to help the environment, campaign finance laws must be put in tune with long-term ecological reasoning.

Even more pervasive among economists and politicians is the concept of unlimited economic growth inherited from Adam Smith and others. Modern corporations are the institutional realization of this belief. Unlimited corporate growth is not a natural condition of corporations. It is instead a political choice enshrined in corporate bylaws. The resulting endless economic growth of many successful corporations has contributed to a

transfer of sovereignty from governments to corporate ownership and the consequent privatization of all forms of commons.
A number of corporations are now so large and powerful that
they, rather than politicians, are able to determine law and policy.
They can determine the legal environment of their own activity by
lobbying for legislation or investing a tremendous amount in lawyers and litigation. For example, the Bayh-Dole Act, adopted by
the United States in 1980 under pressure from the pharmaceutical
industry and subsequently transplanted worldwide, authorizes
universities to co-patent with corporate donors the results of publicly funded research. The social benefits of this common intellectual property are thus transformed into privatized, for-profit assets.[4] Similarly, under corporate pressure, European law has been
recently changed in favor of corporations to allow non-disclosure
of the place of production of food, thus stripping even the ecologically literate consumers of the ability to buy local. (Ironically, the
abolition of the duty to inform about the place of origin has been
hidden in the regulations under the many details on the allergenic
potential of food!)[5]

Overall, the consequences of the mechanistic trap for the
commons are dire. Beyond the more obvious and direct environmental issues, such as pollution, deforestation, or rampant over-
development, we also see the continuous privatization of public
utilities, prisons, schools, academic departments, public radio, TV
stations, and many other infrastructures. Corporations now man-
age many of these formerly public holdings in a purely short-term
extractive fashion.

Unfortunately, the general public is insufficiently aware of this
problem, especially because the integrity of the increasingly corporate media is questionable. Likewise, corporate money, working
in pursuit of corporate interests, jeopardizes even the objectivity of
scientific research.[6] Donations and other financial incentives can
capture universities just as they do politicians. This process does
not require personally dishonest scientists, but can occur through
processes in the scientific community such as academic selection
or journal acceptances, which are carried out within institutions
distorted by the need to attract corporate contributions.

Vested interests have designed this state of affairs.[7] Further, the lack of systemic thinking makes it very difficult to hold decision makers accountable for the consequences of their choices. Most people either do not understand the long-term catastrophic consequences of shortsighted decision-making or, if they do, feel completely helpless, since avenues of influence for individuals, such as electoral ballots, are useless.

The strictly quantitative approach and the reduction of human life to abstract units of labor, performed by utility-maximizing individuals or firms, is the current form of the Cartesian mechanistic vision. Economists participating in maintaining this intellectual status quo become part of the establishment. Thus, private-sector incentives and legal structures that encourage exploitative and shortsighted corporate behavior determine the institutional, legal, and intellectual structure of the present extractive economic order that we call a mechanistic trap.[8]

GLOBAL CAPITALISM

During the last decade of the twentieth century, it was generally recognized that a new world was emerging—a world shaped by new technologies, new social structures, a new economy, and a new culture. *Globalization* became the term used to summarize the extraordinary changes and the seemingly irresistible momentum that were felt by millions of people. Within a few years we became quite used to many facets of globalization.[9] We rely on global communications networks and the World Wide Web for information from around the world; through a variety of social media we can remain in daily touch with widely dispersed friends and loved ones.

Together with these agreeable features of globalization, however, a new form of global capitalism emerged during the 1990s, and its impact on our well-being has been much more problematic. This new global capitalism is profoundly different from the capitalism formed during the Industrial Revolution that was critiqued by Karl Marx. It is also very different from the capitalism based on the theories of John Maynard Keynes (1883–1946), which called for a social contract between capital and labor and for the centralized fine-tuning of the business cycles of national economies, which was the dominant economic model for several decades after World War II.

The outstanding characteristic of our current capitalism is that it is global and faces no alternative anywhere in the world that is more genuinely effective and organized. States, limited as they are by the borders of their jurisdictions, are not strong enough to place limits on the global roaming of extractive corporations.[10] With the acceptance of communist China into the World Trade Organization in 2001, the entire world has become governed by essentially the same set of economic rules and institutions. Unfortunately, these institutions are all equally unsustainable and extractive, in both their private decision making by corporations and their public, short-term decision making by governments.

At the center of global capitalism is a network of financial flows, which the law allows to develop outside of any ethical framework as a consequence of its own structure of extraction. In this new economy, capital works in real time. Its continual movement through global financial networks is facilitated by so-called free-trade rules designed to support continued corporate growth. Corporations pursue this growth relentlessly by promoting excessive consumption and a throwaway economy that is energy and resource intensive, generates waste and pollution, depletes the Earth's natural resources, and ultimately separates people. For instance, the sales of large TV sets and other home entertainment devices encourage people to stay at home and discourage other, more community-building activities.

Such sustained corporate effort toward even more privatization is highly efficient when market consumption and the growth of the gross domestic product are considered, but the impact of the new economy on human well-being has been mostly negative. Analyses by scholars and community leaders reveal a multitude of interconnected, harmful consequences of the capitalist freedom of extraction generated by property law, including increasing social inequality and social exclusion, a breakdown of democracy, more rapid and extensive deterioration of the natural environment, and increasing poverty and alienation.[11]

The new global capitalism, still legally supported by the mechanistic vision of ownership as freedom to occupy untapped resources, has threatened and destroyed local communities around the world. In the pursuit of ill-conceived biotechnology it has invaded the sanctity of life by attempting to turn diversity into monoculture, ecology into engineering, and life itself into a commodity. It has enriched a global elite of financial speculators, entrepreneurs, and high-tech professionals, who are all granted the legally protected freedom of extraction. These people have experienced an unprecedented accumulation of wealth, but the social and environmental consequences have been disastrous.[12] As we saw in the financial crisis of 2008, the financial well-being of people around the world has been severely endangered. The mechanistic legal structure of modernity—with its short-term incentive schemes and its support of unlimited corporate growth—is one of the main driving forces of the current condition.

WEAK GOVERNMENTS AND STRONG CORPORATIONS

Since economic globalization has affected virtually all domains of our social and cultural lives, it is not surprising that it also has had a considerable impact on law. Today, international law is not limited to states. Many more subjects have entered the picture, and the still-dominant vision of an international legal order with states as building blocks no longer reflects reality. Some of the new players are associations of states. Some of these have full global reach (e.g., the United Nation or the World Trade Organization), and others have a more limited territorial reach (e.g., the European Union, North American Free Trade Agreement, or Mercado Común del Sur [Southern Common Market]).

International law has progressively recognized such institutions as legal persons, without producing any fundamental rethinking of the discipline.[13] Since its foundation by Hugo Grotius, international law has remained based on individualized Cartesian building blocks—legal persons in competition with each other within a mechanistic, depoliticized vision of law—rather than being interpreted as a genuine global network of relationships where actual power ratios between and within communities make it impossible to distinguish law from politics. Private corporations, often stronger than governments, are free to roam the globe and are not accountable for violations of international human rights, in contrast to legal limits on governments and their officials. Although corporations are the most powerful de facto actors in international law, capable of determining its content, the lack of an ecological vision of the legal system makes them invisible and shields them from responsibility, just as the East India Company was brilliantly defended by Grotius. Corporate money determines the behavior of states, and often of nongovernmental organizations. For example, corporations have funded the spread of the use of genetically modified organisms (GMOs) in Africa, or the eradication of ancient, community-building cultural practices such as collective land tenure schemes or polygamy.

The expansion of privatization and individualism is the result of a legal structure—the pincer movement of private property and state sovereignty—that does not respect commons and community. Three centuries of transforming commons into capital have weakened governments and the public interest, allowing dominance by strong corporate actors. The boundaries of the states consequently have become porous to the massive and sudden movement of capital, resulting in dramatic social outcomes, such as when the Hungarian tycoon George Soros single-handedly torpedoed various European currencies in 1992, or when massive speculation produced the crisis of the "Asian Tigers" in 1997.[14]

The other well-known consequence of this global power ratio between the two arms of the pincer is the "revolving door phenomenon," which allows leaders to move randomly between the private and the government sectors, generating blatant conflicts of interest. In the United States, an icon of this distortion is former Vice President Dick Cheney, whose relationship with the military-industrial complex played a major role in determining the Iraq war.

Likewise, some members of the economic team of the George W. Bush administration moved back and forth from Goldman Sachs to public office before joining the Obama administration. In Europe, too, various prime ministers and economic ministers have been or have become officers of Goldman or of other investment banks.

The Western legal tradition developed to protect the private economic agent against the government when the government was strong and property owners were weak. It has now produced a major constitutional imbalance, protecting the private against the public rather than the public against the private. This development is the main reason that privatization is rampant globally while nationalization has ceased to be an option. Only private property, not the commons, is legally protected, and government appropriation of commons is not subject to court decisions and is purely discretionary.[15]

Possibly even more than decisions of governments, the decisions of private corporations affect the lives of millions of people today, yet only governments can be legitimized in democratic terms, while corporations are discussed only in terms of economic efficiency. Thus, CEOs can make in a few hours what their employees make in a year of work; this discrepancy is socially unacceptable even if they work for "private" corporations, because such inequality is the first foe of community. The dominant attitude that distinguishes private responsibility from public social responsibility is itself a product of the understanding of the law we need to change. Because any model of an exclusive concentration of power is a foe of the commons and of an ecologically sustainable legal order, a legal system focused on regenerating the commons must address this issue of those who have accumulated too much, thanks to our extractive system of property, and have left others with too little.

However, governments, embedded as they are in global networks of turbulent financial flows, are less and less able to control their national economic policies. They can no longer deliver on the promises of the traditional welfare state, such as free health care and education, unemployment benefits, and so forth. They are fighting a losing battle against a newly globalized criminal economy—a network of powerful organizations engaged in a broad range of criminal activities, from drug trafficking and arms dealing to identity theft and the laundering of billions of dollars. As a result, the authority and legitimacy of governments is becoming more and more questionable.[16]

In addition, the state is disintegrating from within through the corruption of the democratic process. Especially in the United States, political actors increasingly depend on corporations and other lobbying groups to finance electoral campaigns in exchange for policies that favor their special interests. Such regulatory capture is widely documented and explains crucial decisions such as tort reform in the interest of insurance companies or unfair subsidies to corn-producing agro-businesses. But less is known about the impact of corporate money on jurisdiction even at the level of the U.S. Supreme Court. In just the past ten years, this most important court has protected Hollywood's interest in extending the length of intellectual property rights; allowed big pharmaceutical companies to benefit from local tax subsidies in establishing their campuses; shielded the oil industry from the consequences of its environmental damage; and protected financial interests from responsibility for the 2008 crisis.[17] Apparently, no one can significantly control the secret relationships between weak governments and the might of concentrated capital.

SEPARATION OF CAPITAL FROM LABOR

We also have a wealth of detailed analysis of the social and cultural impact of the structure of global capitalism. Indeed, the new global economy has profoundly transformed the social relationships between capital and labor.[18] In global capitalism, money, escaping into the virtual reality of electronic networks, has become almost entirely independent of production and services. Capital is global at its core, while labor, as a rule, is local. Thus, money and people increasingly exist in different spaces and times: in the virtual space of financial flows and in the real local and regional places where people are employed; in the instant time of electronic communications and in the biological time of everyday life. Economic power resides in the global financial networks of extractive corporations, which determine the fate of most jobs, while labor remains locally constrained in the real world, becoming fragmented and disempowered.

As a result, the global is far away, but the only possible field of organized resistance is local. As more and more companies restructure themselves into decentralized networks of smaller units (often exploited by a hierarchical relationship with the parent company), which in turn are linked to networks of suppliers and subcontractors, workers are increasingly employed through individual contracts. Thus labor is losing its collective identity and bargaining power. Many workers today, whether unionized or not, will not fight for higher wages or better working conditions out of fear that their jobs will be moved to another municipality, or even abroad. Indeed, in the new economy, traditional working-class communities have all but disappeared. The deaths of thriving communities such as Detroit or Flint, famously described by Michael Moore in his 1989 documentary *Roger & Me*, are tragic examples of a trend reflected by statistical data that often make the Keynesian compromise between labor and capital a sweet memory from the past.

This grim picture of individualization and disempowerment is not the outcome of some law of nature. Instead, it is the outcome of the extractive legal setting put in place when the need was to transform the abundant commons into capital that at the time was too scarce. This legal setting is based in a particular conception of property law, based on the assumed freedom to extract resources and exploit labor.

PRIVATE PROPERTY AND EXCLUSION

The absence of an alternative to the mechanistic vision became clear in the aftermath of the financial crisis of 2008, when the only proposal that actually passed, the Troubled Asset Relief Program, was just a gigantic transfer of public money to corporate institutions that were deemed "too big to fail." Readers who consider this program successful because of some signs of "recovery" in the U.S. economy are exactly those whom this book is trying to awaken from the utopian idea that back-to-business-as-usual and economic growth are either possible or desirable. Some broader proposals made in the spirit of Keynesian regulation and government intervention—genuine government control following bailouts, nationalization of private interests, and increased taxation to finance public spending—were defeated before even being attempted. Governments simply do not have the teeth to bite the corporations. They can only bark. In the late 1970s and early 1980s, Margaret Thatcher and Ronald Reagan had advocated addressing the failure of "too much state" with more free market; in the aftermath of the 2008 crisis, it seemed to some well-intentioned people that the failure of too much free market had to be addressed by more state intervention. Because this zero-sum game between market and state is part of the problem rather than part of the solution, it is not surprising that public and private interests worked together to protect CEO compensation schemes against the government and potential global regulators.

The catastrophic global economic meltdown was brought about by Wall Street bankers through a combination of greed, incompetence, and weaknesses inherent in the system.[19] In seeking approval for a bank bailout of gigantic proportions, President Obama, new in office, asserted that he was going to involve government only under the condition of responsible cuts of CEO compensation packages. Less than twenty-four hours after his statement, however, the president was forced by the corporate powers represented in his economic team—the same bankers who had served under President Bush—to recant. Without any apparent embarrassment, Obama stated that in a society governed by the rule of law, contracts already entered into were untouchable. In other words, the president had to bow to the "natural laws" of the market.[20]

At the moment, however, no such legal protection is available for the commons—the natural and cultural resources of communities—which can be privatized, expropriated, or damaged without just compensation or any due process of law. Unfortunately, as the Occupy movement of 2011 pointed out, a genuine alternative to a market capitalism that protects the interests of the 1 percent cannot be found in a government elected by the money of that 1 percent. We still need to develop a systemic vision of the public interest that is rooted in a robust legal protection of the commons—not an ideological confusion between the public interest and the government.

The current legal structure, based on the concentration of power and exclusion, provided no alternative solution to the crisis. Such exclusion is another intrinsic feature of global capitalism, a direct consequence of the fact that its network structure, by design, lacks any ethical framework. As the flows of capital and information interlink worldwide networks of individual property rights, all populations and territories on the periphery are denied subjectivity and reduced to targets of financial gain. As a result, certain segments of societies, areas of cities, regions, and even entire countries become economically victimized as objects of plunder. They are not recognized as participants and their opinions are excluded from the debate.

The unifying principle of social exclusion remains the institution of private property, the building block of our Western legal tradition. Based on a mechanistic vision of the relationship between humans and nature, property law is still perhaps the most powerful institution of exclusion, individualization, and competitive accumulation. The "No Trespassing" sign, ubiquitous in the United States, is the symbol of the sovereign rule of owners over their property. Private ownership of land excludes many people from access to and enjoyment of nature and denies many others the right to produce healthy, safe food locally and sustainably. Even animals are considered objects of property, and the fact that they are sensitive beings is simply disregarded for the sake of the food industry and manufacturing.

Nor is privatization neutral toward the development of public spaces. Public transportation is reduced by the spread of private cars, with negative ecological and social effects. Public phones are almost unavailable now that most people have private cell phones. Public education simply cannot endure competition from private corporate actors, as is particularly evident in the United States, where public universities are now unreasonably expensive and advertise and engage in branding as if they were shoe factories.[21] The outrageous prices that U.S. hospitals charge for services is largely determined by pharmaceutical corporations' hefty drug prices. As a result, many people today file bankruptcy and even become homeless because of medical debts, which is possibly the most immoral aspect of what sociologist Andy Ross has recently called "creditocracy."[22] A legal and economic machinery is in place by which the people remain under the yoke of debt, with no possibility of repaying it in the course of their lifetime. Corporate-captured bankruptcy law has gone so far as to make personal bankruptcy unavailable for student loans, so that an entire generation has to "use its Visa to pay its MasterCard," a consequence of the individualistic idea that a young human being studies hard only for himself (typically competing with others for future higher pay). In fact, education is a typical common, because better-educated people contribute to a better society for all.

The tight structural connection between private property and unsustainable practices of short-term extraction explains the difficulty of exiting the mechanistic trap. The law severely limits our ability to take into account the effect of current economic decisions on future generations or the true costs of unsustainable activities for the community at large. As we have discussed, mechanisms of liability embedded in corporate charters force managers to pursue the bottom line and shareholder value. Moreover, property law protects even the most irrational individualistic and selfish behavior. In the law, the Romantic critique of Cartesian rationalism accused it of promoting a standardized reasonable man, which only produced more individualist bias. Legal systems only very reluctantly recognize the notion of an abuse of right, so that upstream owners can deprive downstream ones of the flow of clean water, no matter how the social utility of their two usages compares. Similarly, land developers can obstruct neighboring buildings from access to sunlight, even if access to solar energy would be a much sounder interest from the ecological point of view. On a more general scale, proprietary freedom includes practices such as fracking, which endangers communities for unclear gain, mostly in the form of corporate subsidies. Systemically irrational behaviors (such as the practice of monoculture for fuel production, which consumes as much water and soil to produce one tank of gas as would be needed to sustain the life of one person for one year) are all free exercise of proprietary power and freedom of contract.

Any attempt to put public interest over private ownership faces a high burden of proof, because scores of economists, jurists, and pundits immediately rush to protect the sanctity of private property and the unlimited freedom of an owner.[23] Regulation of private property is always the exception in the Western legal tradition, and the default rule remains unrestrained freedom. Above all, property law protects corporations—all-powerful, eternal institutions that are structurally incapable of generosity or ethical behavior.

HIERARCHY AND COMPETITION

As we have seen, the mechanistic trap promotes a vision of the legal system as an aggregate of pre-existing legal rules that abstractly bind everybody, both the weak and the strong. This ideology makes plain, law-abiding people think of law almost as if it were a set of instructions to assemble a potentially dangerous appliance. The law must be strictly followed, out of fear of an explosion or other mishap. It also reflects the notion of "mechanical jurisprudence," in which the legal system is seen as a machine applying a hierarchy of norms to the concrete facts of a situation in a predictable and constant manner with no injection of creativity by an interpreter.

Lawyers, however, know that no legal system *really* works this way, but they keep this idea as an initiated secret in order to protect their turf. Since the late nineteenth century, the French jurist François Gény (1861–1959) and many others following his lead have drawn attention to the creative role of the interpreter who invariably introduces his or her own value judgments in applying the law.[24] Gény's contemporary, long-term Italian conservative Prime Minster Giovanni Giolitti (1842–1928), used to say that the law is interpreted for friends but applied to enemies. The necessities and complexities of legal practice led some legal scholars to recognize the role of the interpreter's subjectivity well before a similar observation was made in quantum theory, although this observation remained at best a partial critique; it was never developed as a total critique, or paradigm shift, in the general understanding of the nature of law.[25] The idea that the weak and the strong are equally bound by abstract rules still holds sway as a powerful ideology in spite of so much contrary evidence.

According to a more realist legal vision, the last word in the law does not belong to the legal professionals at the top of the pyramid, such as a supreme court. Rather, it belongs to those at the bottom, because the usual decision maker is the one closest to the actual conflict, the interpreter who actually captures (or makes) the law in action in most cases. This realist image is not unlike the situation in quantum physics, where knowledge is based only on probability because the observer determines what he can observe. In this same sense, knowledge of the law can only be probabilistic because we do not really know where the law is at any given moment except when we capture it by adjudication. Thus, the outcome of a legal conflict is not predictable with certainty (as the mechanistic vision claims) but is only probable, since we are not able to master all the factors that determine the prejudices of the interpreter.[26]

Over time, this observation has had an impact on the very theory of the sources of the law: the different authorities (constitution, international treaties, statutes, judicial precedents, and legal writings) that lawyers use in their reasoning. Competition among sources of law, as an alternative to the previous hierarchical vision, emerged as the most important metaphor in the last part of the twentieth century when, after the fall of the socialist alternative, neo-liberal theories of law famously stated that the law should be market friendly.[27] The triumph of economics among the social sciences, combined with a variety of neo-Darwinian evolutionary ideas, made jurists believe that the legal system naturally evolves toward economic efficiency. Less-efficient rules—those that are not in tune with what market actors would do if they were free to negotiate among themselves a solution—are challenged through litigation and ultimately discarded.

In this way, an *instrumental* vision of law as a tool to make social organization more efficient and productive has gained global currency as the consensus of those who view human law as a technology. It has produced a legal mindset particularly keen on seeing competition instead of hierarchy as the way in which the machine of justice should operate, separated from the irrationalities of the political process and of the localized needs of communities: a depoliticized, technocratic vision of law. The eventual triumph of the idea of a spontaneous market order as the law of a free society has made competition the metaphor for open legal systems—that is, legal systems based on market democracy, the rule of law, and global communication in the international marketplace.

However, although this notion of competition de-legitimizes hierarchy as a desirable form of social ordering, it also reflects the reductionist approach to human laws, based as it is on a vision of individualized actors competing for an outcome: the generation of a legal order more friendly to discrete individual interest. Thus, the state or the private owner is still at the center of the legal order, though today the private owner may be a transnational corporation capable of a global reach.

Today, for the first time since the birth of the modern state, the private sector is stronger than the government.[28] The result is a seemingly irreversible machine that produces inequality and ecological disaster following the very structure of property rights. The mechanistic and abstract vision of the law has helped to progressively expropriate resources from the 99 percent in favor of the 1 percent. No ecological order would sustain such a degree of inequality. A return to more government bureaucracy is not the solution. Attempts to cure the excesses of competition with new hierarchy, as was done by the mainstream in the aftermath of the global 2008 crisis by means of government bailouts, are of no practical use. A movement from one mechanistic alternative to the other is simply bound to end up with more plunder and more of the same failed policy. In order to solve our systemic problems, we need a total critique that leads out of the mechanistic trap. This is provided by an ecological understanding of law.

CHAPTER 8

From Capital to Commons

The Ecological Transformation in Law

B ecause of the tremendous might of the mechanistic trap, an irresistible evolution toward disorder and destruction, as predicted by the second law of thermodynamics, seems unavoidable in human affairs. This grim picture of the world as a machine running down because of immutable mechanical human laws can produce disempowerment and despair unless we realize that, like the laws of nature, human laws are not necessarily cast in the mechanistic vision that currently dominates the common understanding. Moving beyond the current common understanding thus requires a long-term strategy to make the systemic paradigm shift politically relevant. In this chapter, we discuss three strategic objectives to pursue: disconnecting law from power and violence; making community sovereign; and making ownership generative.

DISCONNECTING LAW FROM POWER AND VIOLENCE

The most important structural solution to the rush toward final disorder is to restore some harmony between human laws and the laws of nature by giving law back to networks of communities. If the people were to understand the nature of law as an evolving common, reflecting local conditions and fundamental needs, they would care about it. People would understand that the law is too important to remain in the hands of organized corporate interests.[1] We are the makers and users of the law. If we are *alone* in front of the law, we are inevitably afraid. However, *together* we are the law! We must understand that the only real power we have as individuals and communities is to choose how to look at the law in the community. Do we recognize it as fair and legitimate in the broader goal to save civilization? Do we decide to abide by it or not? How much are we willing to put ourselves at stake to avoid what Hannah Arendt called the banality of evil?[2] We do not need to be heroes—we only need to develop an ecological perception of society. We need a vision that defeats economic-induced individualism by locating the law at the level of social networks and ecological communities. We need, as a society, to pierce the ideological veil of a legal system that is abstract and mechanical, "owned" by the state, and kept distant from individual people by the professionalized culture of corporate lawyers.

To accomplish such empowerment, human communities must challenge the mechanistic vision that makes us perceive the law as an objective system, "out there," based on concentrated power, and interpreted only in its own terms by means of artificial, professionally transmitted knowledge. The current vision of the law as an a priori order against which all social activity can be judged in the abstract, as either legal or illegal, is the opposite of a holistic vision of law, which sees law as a constantly negotiated process of making cultural connections, as is required by systemic thinking.

In the view of evolutionist and Romantic jurists, the law reflects the felt needs of society, the spirit of the people, rather than the needs of state or corporate actors. As we know, global capitalism has hijacked this promising vision. Today, we should not locate the spirit of the people in the old professional law books (whether of Roman law or of the common law); rather, we should genuinely look into the social wealth generated by the good practices, desires, and visions of the 99 percent, in order to protect them against corporate and government expropriation. For example, understanding the true social costs of patenting publicly funded research, not only in terms of excluding people from the benefits of medical research but also in terms of the future freedom of scientific research, may inspire communities to resist—not only campus activists, but communities at large. Community lawyers who are fully aware of the long-term consequences of extractive law can challenge the substantive legitimacy of the Bayh-Dole Act or of the many other corporate-driven products of top-down mechanistic law. Similarly, understanding the true ecological costs of the mechanistic structure of responsibility in contractual outsourcing, as exemplified by the Rana Plaza tragedy, may trigger similar global resistance by a variety of means such as boycotts of extractive global brands or development of new doctrines of responsibility. Having an awareness of the ideological nature of dominant discourses about the law will allow communities to produce politically viable solutions.

Such a shared vision of law, once it becomes part of the common understanding, would oppose professional interests whose profit stems from alienating the law from its makers, users, and interpreters. It would perceive people not as individualized abstractions, but rather as functioning in complex networks of quality-based social and ecological relationships, like all other living creatures. It would generate quality-based human laws that, like the ecological laws of nature, would create further social resources and value rather than extract existing value.

In opposition to this vision, the dominant common understanding based on legal and political professionalism expropriates the inherent capacity of these common networks to generate law. For example, the idea that the private sector is more efficient than the government sector has gained political currency along bipartisan lines. Intellectual property law has helped businesses to benefit from such ideological investment, whereas unpatented cultural and natural resources, which generate other, nonmarket resources, do not count as part of the gross domestic product. Commons-based alternatives to privatization—such as prizes, grants, scholarships to authors or producers, or crowdfunding of shared projects—have been insufficiently explored as alternatives to intellectual property regimes. This paradoxical system, which justifies fundamentally exclusionary corporate ownership in order to generate socially beneficial knowledge, though increasingly denounced,[3] remains part of the common worldview. Consequently, ancient cultures based on sharing collective knowledge, such as the Chinese culture, are singled out as lacking a "rule of law" because of the reluctant enforcement of intellectual property.[4] Most seriously, people who resist such enclosures of knowledge are deemed pirates and prosecuted, rather than being recognized as heroes of the 99 percent. (The tragedy of Aaron Swartz, who took his own life at the age of twenty-seven, during his fight for the commons, must never be forgotten.)[5]

As we have seen, the historical accumulation of professional knowledge, rooted in mechanistic thinking and serving the interests of capital accumulation, determines the current common worldview. Obviously, transforming this established view is not easy. A first necessary step is to challenge the dominant professionalized vision of the legal order as being separate from its communities of users and makers.

An ecological understanding of law, the only revolution possible through culture and genuine civic engagement, overcomes both hierarchy and competition as "correct" narratives of the legal order. It seeks to capture the complex relationships among the parts and the whole—between individual entitlements, duties, rights, power, and the law—by using the metaphor of the network and of the open community sharing a purpose. Ultimately, we need a paradigm shift, a total critique that, in the name of recovering Gaia, places the living Earth once again at the center of the legal perspective and returns the law into the hands of active communities. The mechanistic relationship between individuals in market competition or state hierarchy can be overcome only by the bottom-up emergence of new, context-specific, community-based "natural laws," now understood as principles of ecology that have allowed life on Earth to flourish for billions of years.

This move, instead of limiting human agency to decide what laws will govern our social organizations, is simply a shift away from both individual and state-centric approaches; a shift from the violent logic of domination and consumption that is inherent in both hierarchy and competition; a generalized recognition that public and private law, as conceived today, represent false alternatives, since both are metaphors of exclusion and concentration of power in pursuit of growth. We need a new legal vision of an ecological community that negotiates its own laws in a genuine forward-looking political conversation, free from the ideological baggage of modernity.

For example, when a group of people has a shared purpose— such as recovering an abandoned factory, which famously happened in Argentina after the default—they can self-organize for the best possible pursuit of their goal. They divide labor according to capabilities; they brainstorm for best solutions; they evaluate individual proposals; they develop shared ideas of internal fairness; they organize mechanisms for dispute resolution; they seek cooperation with fellow workers in similar situations; they need and seek appreciation from neighboring communities in order to resist the power of the official law.[6] Neither hierarchy nor competition captures the concept of such legal organizations. Such communities diffuse power and practice inclusion by means of an interiorized, self-enforcing legal system based on a communality of values and purpose. Mechanistic law based on concentrated power, in contrast, has proved incapable of any reaction other than the use of violence, deemed legitimate in its own terms.

Instead of being alienated from the law governing them, the participants in these enterprises are their own law-givers and enforcers; they stand outside of any power concentration and or any claim of monopoly over violence. They overcome the artificial distinction between a private and a public sphere of their lives. Interpretation of law is here a nonprofessional exercise in the sharing of collective meaning. Law, when it is separated from depending on power and violence, is like language, culture, or the arts: it becomes a way through which a collectivity communicates and decides about itself. Much as the premises of an old, abandoned factory are a physical common returning to life, similarly the law returns to life in the daily experience of these workers, allowing them to generate an ecological, sustainable adaptability to the needs and circumstances of their struggle.

There is no reason to believe that, as a species in a collective struggle for our future, we cannot organize in a network of similar generative legal orders, a large bottom-up network of autonomous political, social, and economic communities that prosper in social production and reproduction outside of the ideological distinction between what is private and what is public. There is no reason to believe that we cannot go beyond abstraction to give practical and political relevance to a new, systemic understanding translated into a new legal vision that allows us to survive and prosper.

MAKING COMMUNITY SOVEREIGN

The dominant vision of modernity is that the Scientific Revolution awakened humankind from the "dark ages," allowing it to dominate both its own future and nature by transforming commons into capital. As an unfortunate result, the majority of today's urban inhabitants are disconnected from nature, mired in ecological illiteracy and alienation. For the first time in human history, more than half of the world's population lives in an urban setting.[7] Most children do not experience seasons through the transformation of plants or animals (except as domestic pets), and they know nothing about the production of the food that they see packaged in refrigerators, because most people do not grow their own food. Western people spend a lot of time indoors, drive everywhere, and assume that water comes out of the faucet as a matter of course. Urban people in rich countries exercise their "right" to take long showers, even when there are severe droughts in places such as California. They also like to keep the air-conditioning on all the time during the summer, the lights on in the skyscrapers at night, and even keep the engine on in their gas-gulping SUVs when they stop to chat with a friend or wait for their kids in front of schools. If someone objects to this practice the simple answer is, "This is my gas!" or "I pay for my water and energy!," so "Mind your own business!" These consumption habits, which many people do not even notice, are tragic. The energy output of the nuclear reactor of Fukushima, Japan, responsible for a major disaster in the spring of 2011, was so low in relative terms that as much energy as it produced could be easily saved by switching off the lights of Tokyo at night. (Some fifty nuclear reactors in Japan produce only 30 percent of the total energy consumption of the country, so that each reactor produces only about 0.6 percent of the total!)[8] Taking on the risks of a nuclear plant (whose leftovers take 180,000 years to stop being dangerous) in order to overuse electricity for urban life in rich countries does not seem like a rational behavior for a species that claims to have exited from the Dark Ages! All such behaviors are examples of a proprietary individualism that, instead of having freed us from medieval superstition, has produced an irrational idolatry for selfish entitlement.

Part of the remedy for this alienation of urbanized people from nature may be to create and protect areas that ban ownership and exclusion from forests and other natural spaces, allowing people to reconnect with the commons and with their historic relation to nature. Examples of "trespass-free" legal systems already exist, even in the capitalist world. For instance, the Scandinavian "right to roam" laws ban landowners from excluding people from the land. Although Scandinavian countries do recognize the right of property on land, they also consider it very important to foster broad access to nature for ecological and health purposes. Consequently, owners in the countryside, of a garden, of a private park, or of uncultivated land, have no right to fence it.[9] Everybody has the right to enter that land in an unobstructed way, and owners are legally responsible for ensuring safe and open access to their private land. People even have the right to camp on someone else's land for a reasonable period of time and can only be excluded from the immediate premises of the owners' home dwelling.

In the Western legal tradition, a variety of other property rights structures can be interpreted to allow for the direct occupation of property and to protect its generative use. Legal structures such as community land trusts, deployed in a number of cities in the United States and in Europe to revamp blighted property, can be used to vest property rights in a community for extensive areas; individuals are only allowed exclusive property rights to some portions that they are permitted to refurbish for themselves. They must inhabit the premises and they cannot sell or rent their property. As members of the community, they participate in the running of the trust. The community, a notion that includes future generations, is thus the beneficiary of a trust, and individuals might have rights of exclusive use with various limitations on whether they can transfer parts of it. The community land trust is quite an effective institution in limiting the impact of rent extraction for low-income people.[10] Its governance is vested in trustees who are selected in a variety of ways, usually by community assembly. Similarly, the "public trust doctrine" has limited the ability of governments in office to develop wild areas or other nature,[11] and community foundations can deploy a similar function in the civil law tradition to protect cultural property and heritage. However, such doctrines are still exceptions, never addressed as possible full-fledged alternatives in basic property law—although recent litigation brought by teenage plaintiffs in Oregon shows the promise of broadly conceptualizing the law regarding the rights of future generations to have the atmosphere recognized as a common in public trust.[12]

Elsewhere, property law can be structured in such a way that absentee property owners lose their property rights to actively cultivating occupants. Legal systems can do so by using very short terms for so-called adverse possession or by allowing young farmers, organized in cooperatives, to petition local governments when they are interested in cultivating portions of land that they identify as vacant. The local government can then grant a provisional title that, after a couple of years, can evolve into property.

Property also can be vested in foundations carrying on the interest of future generations, or in other innovative legal institutions, such as those deployed in some of the worker-managed factories in Argentina, Greece, France, Italy, and Turkey.[13] In these instances, as workers are producing everything from organic foods to tiles, from high-quality ice cream to construction equipment, the structures of governance are struggling to become more inclusive and sophisticated than traditional cooperative assemblies.[14] Decision making is not limited to workers but involves special boards that give local stakeholders or friends who help generate the needed funds a right to participate in the assembly.

Developing tenure systems characterized by their generative capacity and that favor sustainable production over rent extraction is perhaps the most important frontier of property law. Translating capital and technology into commons requires an ecological legal order based upon genuine respect and a common purpose, which each community would be able to interpret and apply according to its own cultural traditions, business opportunities, and shared desires.

In the rhetoric of modernity, private property is a "despotic domain" that lasts "forever," unless the owner transfers it.[15] When an owner disposes of property in favor of another owner, what was previously a common is thus transformed into capital as exchange value. Transfers of individual ownership back into the commons do not generate capital. That can happen only under the most exceptional circumstances through the mechanism of state sovereignty. A radical revision of property and of its relationship with state sovereignty is thus necessary if we wish to transform capital back into commons and build an ecological legal order. Such an alternative begins with the understanding that a community lives and unfolds in a common space where the actions of one member affect the well-being of all others. Such space is the venue of life and death for a community and it must serve the interest of every one of its members, regenerating life in it. Whereas extractive institutions progressively transform the life of community into death, first socially and later also physically, generative institutions produce incentives for regeneration.

In face-to-face communities where everybody has knowledge of the community's laws, customs, and uses, opportunistic extractive and selfish behavior, while certainly not absent, is collectively monitored.[16] Individuals seeking social approval and peer recognition are encouraged to recognize and care for the common space. An example would be a sound academic community, where individual scholars are encouraged to do socially useful or academically prestigious work that increases the reputation of the whole faculty, rather than engaging in private for-profit consulting or business practices whose reputational value might be very high economically for the individual but modest if not negative ecologically for the group.

In an ecological legal order the community, not the individual or the state, is sovereign. The sovereign community can recognize private property provided it is generative and serves a living purpose (an example would be providing for low-income individual use in a community land trust); otherwise, the community must have the full power to revoke private property that, being extractive, is something like a public nuisance. This philosophy lies behind the power of expropriation for non-use, which is reluctantly recognized in some legal systems; it is a solution to be expanded and vested in the hands of communities of potential users.

Innovative institutional solutions, such as a jury of the commons deciding on the use of blighted property, are emerging to face the crisis-induced housing emergency in some local Italian municipalities. Another possibility, experienced in the United States for limiting regulation, is the use of sunset laws. Sunset provisions for individual property rights, so that they expire and return to the commons at a given time or at the occurrence of certain incidents, are ideal compromises in the difficult trade-off between individualism and community. The living community, which is the real sovereign over the common space, can transfer some of this space to a member or members as private property, so long as the transfer itself is generative. Similarly, a social contract to concentrate power in the hands of a leader makes sense only as long as such a concentration serves the interest of all. In this sense, any institutional arrangement concerning a territory must remain conditional upon the living purpose of the ecological community, which involves all the living and those yet to be born. When the living purpose is abandoned, the institutional setting behind it must also be abandoned, in an effort to elaborate a new, more ecologically legitimate order.

The same conditionality, more controversial because it entails a radical challenge to constituted authority, is true of public sovereignty.[17] The state is a legitimate institution from the ecological perspective only so long as it is capable of protecting the community against the extractive use of private property. Indeed, the boundaries between private property and the commons are always negotiated though the state. Because the commons are the direct expression of the sovereign community within a territory, a legitimate state cannot protect them less intensively than it protects private property. If the protection that state institutions offer to the commons is weaker than that granted to private property (as is the case in Western constitutional law), then the state itself lacks legitimacy. In such a case, the community faces a collective duty to resist extraction by a direct challenge to extractive property arrangements.

Communities of citizens can organize themselves by entering pacts to share the care of the commons with municipal authorities, which provide a variety of material means to facilitate these different endeavors. A European network of resisting local communities has developed to link together the commons movement in Spain, Italy, Greece, Germany, France, and many other places. The willingness to engage with representative politics has determined a new phase in the European movements, which are counterparts to the Occupy movement in the United States that has been reluctant to seek political representation. The European social movements have a shared sense about what to do if they wind up occupying the political institutions: power will be decentralized back to smaller-scale communities, facilitating the birth of new institutions of the commons.

In Spain, a brand-new political organization, Podemos, which stems directly from the May 15, 2011, *acampada* (protest camping) of Puerta del Sol, is now projected to have 27 percent of the general vote, making it the leading Spanish party prior to the 2016 general political elections. Podemos has developed around an agenda of struggle (*La Plataforma*) against the half million foreclosures carried on by banks in Spain through unfair practices condemned by the European Court of Justice. The platform has collected 1.5

million signatures to introduce in Parliament a bill based on the concept of "social rent," an arrangement by which tenants will pay for foreclosed and empty housing units in proportion to what they can afford. In Spain today 3.5 million empty new apartments have been built because of German and French speculation.

In Greece, a similar loose coalition of different political and social organizations, known as Syriza, became the leading political party in the 2015 elections. Syriza was born in the process of resistance to the country's austerity policies and the consequent massive privatizations forced by the European Commission, the International Monetary Fund, and the Central European Bank (the so-called Troika). Its leader is now the prime minister, and its political platform, embattled by the established powers, stems from the bottom up in a continuous dialogue with local communities and social movements.

The tactic of seeking political representation is not a contradiction *per se* for the commons, even if the hierarchical structure of political parties and the competitive nature of the electoral process make it insufficient as a strategy. Ecological communities develop around negotiated consent, not by majority rule (especially if the majority of participants is indeed a small minority, as in most Western political elections).

MAKING OWNERSHIP GENERATIVE

Today we must understand the legal foundations of old and current generative practices to regain control of a mechanistic rule of law that has produced private monsters taking over the very governments that have created them. (In the United States the Supreme Court decision on *Citizens United v. Federal Election Commission* has all but officially transferred the electoral process over to corporations.) Ancient institutions of the commons that provide communities with water, wood, agricultural products, education, and housing construction are still alive in ecological niches in Europe and are still very important in much of Africa, South Asia, and Latin America.[18] Typically, these institutions are based on exchanges of labor performed by individuals organized in age groups. In the European Alps, for example, one age group would cut and season logs for use after two, sometimes three, generations. In some places such collective practices, organized in participatory institutional settings, generate important economic support for the community. The wood that supports many buildings of Venice was so wonderfully seasoned by the nearby *Magnifica Comunità di Fiemme* (a commons institution) in nearby Trentino that it has lasted in the lagoon since the sixteenth century. Before colonization, India had developed highly sophisticated decentralized networks of aqueducts and channels that were perfectly coherent with the local ecology. This system provided water of a quality for consumption and irrigation that has never been matched by the mechanistic system of big dams and pipes built by the English in support of their extractive economy; and the latter system has been responsible for many droughts.

Even today, when a common need emerges, people tend to organize in common to run recuperated spaces, factories, theaters, gardens, farmers markets, or institutions such as Time Banks. In such institutions, quickly developing in many countries, people make their time available to others for babysitting, elder care, household work, moving, or other similar activities, thus "depositing" time that they can then "withdraw" when they have needs. Quite a number of communities have also developed local currencies, for exchanges of services within the community.[19]

In urban settings, the need for quality food has led to people entering agreements with farmers to pay money for organic food production with a fair margin for labor, in exchange for receiving the seasonal products when ready, according to their specific needs. These simple collective institutions are highly virtuous from an ecological perspective, because they avoid both waste in consumption and the exploitation of farmers by big agribusiness in production. In the Italian experience, the *Gruppi di Acquisto Solidale* (groups of buying in solidarity) are not limited to farming products; they can be extended to tailor-produced clothing and different kinds of quality artisan manufacture. The Internet has facilitated the formation of such ecological communities in large European cities, and it is likely that, in the future, an increased share of exchanges based on solidarity and shared needs will escape the extractive logic of modern agriculture.

These emerging alternatives, based on the recognition of common needs, material or spiritual, make us understand that the resources necessary to satisfy a need must themselves be understood as a common and governed according to the principles of solidarity necessary for all to satisfy their needs and for the community to prosper. Such a governing activity, known as *commoning*, not only cares for the existing commons but also generates new ones, because people exchange ideas and opportunities when they do things together.[20] Commoning practices, inherited from the past and adapted to current needs, must become the new default rules to deploy whenever the modern property-sovereignty arrangement fails to prove itself generative and in the public interest. Ecological law is a bridge to the future based on experimentation and on learning from mistakes, past as well as present.

Whereas most commoning practices are local, some needs, such as those satisfied by culture and knowledge, share an important global dimension. Knowledge that is capable of facing current challenges cannot afford to be parochial, and thus social networks, powerfully facilitated by the Internet, are extremely important. Moreover, in the current political system the relevant decision making is global, because currently the strongest political actors are the global corporations. To counterbalance their influence, different communities must assume their global political role through networking and sharing experiences, thus constructing the foundations for an international legal order based on independent, legally organized commons.

This is not an abstract concept. In the course of its struggle with the owners, a recovered, worker-run factory, because it is technically illegal, will face problems of access to funds, needed machinery, or even utilities. It will also need a market for its products. It will be able to thrive, perhaps using an alternative currency, a different banking system, or different solidarity agreements with other similarly spirited commons. Such a factory will be eager to network with other organizations by sharing its vision; having received solidarity, it will likely support new experiences of a similar kind. Through this networking, an alternative economy will gradually emerge, progressively subtracting spaces from the extractive logic of capitalism.

A generative ecological law will support this economy, a network from the local to the global. However, the official extractive legal system will fight it through the use of mechanistic law as organized violence. The Spanish government, for instance, is now passing laws precluding *acampadas* and solidarity with immigrants and the poor, and increasing sanctions for occupations—all the kinds of activities that would be encouraged by an ecological vision of law. Until these new networks are robust enough to generate ecological law both locally and globally, transnational corporations will be unchecked in their propagation of international legal disorder of the lethal kind we experienced in the crisis of 2008. In the current global institutional setting, it is naïve to believe that governments will ever act in the interest of the people or of the long-term survival of the planet.

Business journalist Marjorie Kelly spent ten years looking at community-owned businesses and other new ownership designs around the world.[21] She concludes that "we are now at the beginning of an ownership revolution." The examples she studied include worker-owned businesses operating "green" laundries, installing solar panels, and producing food in urban greenhouses, as well as the largest department store chain in the United Kingdom, owned 100 percent by its employees; wind farms in Denmark operated by "wind guilds," created by small investors; community land trusts, in which individual families own their homes and a community nonprofit owns the land beneath the homes, thus prohibiting speculative real estate holdings; an organic dairy company in Wisconsin owned by 1,700 farm families; marine fisheries with catch shares that have halted or reversed catastrophic declines in fish stock; cooperatives and nonprofits in Latin America forming a "solidarity economy" to protect communities and ecosystems;

conservation easements covering tens of millions of acres that allow land to be used and farmed while being protected from development; and countless community banks, credit unions, and other varieties of customer-owned banks, thriving amid the financial crisis.

What all these ownership designs have in common is that they create and maintain conditions for human and ecological communities to flourish. Kelly calls this new kind of ownership "generative ownership," and she contrasts it with the "extractive ownership" of the conventional corporate ownership model, whose central feature is maximum financial extraction. In fact, she points out that "our industrial-age civilization has been powered by twin processes of extraction: extracting fossil fuels from the Earth and extracting financial wealth from the economy."[22] Generative ownership, by contrast, serves the needs of life by having the tendencies to be socially just and ecologically sustainable built into the very fabric of its organizational structures. It generates well-being and real, living wealth of the kind we need for transforming capital into commons.

CHAPTER 9

The Commons as a Legal Institution

A systemic revolution in the social domain requires legal institutions producing incentives for the ecologically sustainable behavior of individuals. In order to regenerate relationships, this new institutional framework must avoid concentrating power, but rather diffuse it through ecological community. It must reject selfish accumulation and any exploitation of resources belonging to all. The commons is emerging as such an institution.[1]

THE COMMONS AND THE COMMONING RELATIONSHIP

There is no recognized legal definition of the commons. However, scholars broadly agree that the commons are neither private nor public. Nor are they understood as a commodity, as an object, or as a portion of the material or immaterial space that an owner, private or public, can put on the market to obtain their so-called exchange value. The commons are recognized as such by a community that engages in their management and care not only in its own interest but also in that of future generations.

In fact, as well-known property-law scholar Stefano Rodotà put it, the commons are the opposite of property.[2] Moreover, in the legal philosophy that is now emerging, which is reflected in contemporary co-housing experiences as well as in old village arrangements, so-called private property is actually only an exception to the commons, granted according to variable needs. For example, when children are grown and move out, a household needs one fewer bedroom. Should elderly parents move in, the household then needs an additional room for them. In such cases, if property taken from the commons (for example, a revamped monastery or the buildings of a co-housing project) is temporarily privatized and placed in the care and control of one person, this does not result in accumulation. When these spaces are no longer needed for private use, they must return to the common holding for communal care and use. Thus, the commons are the foe not of individual property but only of the excesses of its accumulation. Similarly, they are not the foe of government. They aim to limit only the excessive concentrations of power by direct decisions made by the community, through correcting feedback loops.[3] Feedback is important, but elected political institutions are typically too remote from where their decisions have impact and individual politicians are too busy to properly decide everything.

A common may be anything a community recognizes as capable of satisfying some real, fundamental need outside of market exchange. In addition to physical public space, this may also include institutional organizations such as cooperatives or commonwealths, trusts in the interest of future generations, village economies, water-sharing devices, and many other arrangements, antique as well as current. Its utility is created by shared community access and diffuse decision making. These commons institutions, through face-to-face reciprocal monitoring, mentoring, and support, tend to counteract the profit motive, inequality, and shortsightedness.

Commons institutions function through the direct legal empowerment of their members in common pursuit of a generative meaning or task, and they respond to real human needs for participation, security, and sociability. Working from the bottom up, such institutions have the potential to take over the core of the legal system, representing a network that can conquer the world not through violence and brutality but through cooperation and partnerships. Because commoners experiment with different models of labor division outside of exploitation, human time is freed up for proselytizing, organizing, and connecting, which allows the network to grow and take over. Government and private property would not necessarily disappear in the ecological legal order, but they would be limited and tamed by the commons.

In the public sphere, a particular physical space may or may not be defined as a common, depending on its use and on whether it is capable of satisfying the fundamental needs of a community, both present and future. For example, although a disused railroad station may be privatized, transformed into a shopping mall, and protected by private police, it also may be recognized and protected as a common, because it is capable of providing shelter to the homeless, a stage for street artists, or a venue for political activism. It does not matter whether the ultimate legal title on the premises is private or public, a corporation or a municipality, only whether the space fosters generative collective activity or is run on a model of exclusion, extracting profit and rent.

The distinction between the public and the private serves only to mask the failure of current democracy. As a society, we locate democracy in the public sphere, where we equate it with electoral practices, and we simply do not care about democracy in the private sphere. We feel entitled to question the organization of this public sphere, but we unquestioningly accept the almost dictatorial structure of modern private corporations. The current legal definitions of private and public actually arise from the same mechanistic logic and, as we have seen, are historically allied against the commons, whereas the separation of public and private does not make any sense when discussing the radically democratic claim of the commons. A commons institution is at the same time legal, political, and economic. The separation between these spheres, as we now know, is just a legacy of mechanistic thinking at the rise of Western capitalism.

By precluding profit extraction, a commons institution frees up a significant amount of resources for social or environmental use (a typical example would be CEO compensation packages). Consequently, running a railroad station as a common can be highly sustainable. The market component of the activity can easily support the nonmarket one: for example, in a community land trust, the rental of expensive space can support low-income housing.

Today, the serious depletion of our common natural and cultural resources makes it imperative that we redress this imbalance of power between the private, the public, and the commons sector. Harmonizing human laws with the principles of ecology requires, at a minimum, the development of a healthy and legally protected commons sector and associated institutions. We must start from the basics of ecological and critical thinking, cultivating diversity, resilience, and social networks capable of changing the world from the bottom up. We can prove in practice not only that commons institutions are morally desirable but also that they are economically sustainable. Governing the world as a quality-based commons rather than as an unlimited reservoir of resources to be extracted will eventually drastically limit the scope of both the business sector, based on private property, and the government sector, based on the might and violence of the military-industrial complex.

Modernity has delegitimized most of the thriving institutions of the commons whose roots in the Western experience date back to early medieval times. Not only the forest and the village in the countryside but also the artisan guilds in the cities—where painters, sculptors, artisans, and notaries learned their skills through long, often harsh, years of apprenticeship—were at the same time legal, political, and economic institutions in historical settings where, as in today's rural villages of the global south, individuals bond with each other in a lifelong relationship of reciprocity and of collective duties to the community. While humanism perhaps justly challenged the oppressive aspects of the old community order in the name of individual self-determination, capitalism has thrown away the baby with the bath water in producing the current lonely crowd. (While loneliness may well be part of the human condition, after the seminal sociological analysis of David Riesman in 1950, it is difficult to argue that it is not also institutionally induced.)[4]

Nostalgia for an order that is long gone is of no use. Nor is it helpful to deny the progress that in many areas, such as medicine, capitalism has brought to some. While many people today, especially in the West, miss a community, nobody misses the quality of pre-modern subsistence farming life. Strong community bonds develop today at any latitude among commoners challenging the established legal order, risking arrest and other sanctions in long-lasting collective struggles to protect a territory from fracking or extraction or a public building from being sold. These bonds can provide the needed twenty-first-century transformation from *homo economicus* into *homo ecologicus*. The brutal break with the medieval consciousness that we described above precluded the gradual development of a commons-based legal system, where jurisprudence could have purified community from its less-than-desirable aspects. A legal notion of *Gemeinschaft* (community) as opposed to *Gesellschaft* (society) was proposed by Ferdinand Tönnies in the nineteenth century but has remained under-theorized.[5] However, other notions, such as that of "sovereignty" or even of "ownership," have had their original harshness limited by elaborations of jurisprudence that reflect social unrest. For example, a variety of doctrines of the separation of powers have limited the power of the sovereign from within by distributing it through different political institutions. There is no reason to believe that this process could not happen with community.

In the current state of affairs, recovering the commons is not the business of lawyers or politicians, whose intellectual and institutional landscape is framed by the ideology of modernity. This process belongs now to plain people who, from choice or necessity, participate in caring for something that they recognize as a common.

In doing so, these people engage in an activity that Nobel laureate Elinor Ostrom describes as "communing."[6] Just as there is no "one-size-fits-all" definition of a common, there can be no such definition of commoning, an activity that one cannot separate from the commons except by deploying the Cartesian idea of separating the subject from the object.

Here we can only introduce some fundamental aspects of commoning, which in different degrees tend to be present wherever such an experience appears. The fundamental organizational principle of commoning everywhere is that of caring, duty, reciprocity, and participation. It is about spending a lot of time together to care for something recognized as a common with high attention and patience. It is a process where individuals sharing a collective purpose institutionalize their collective will to maintain some order and some stability in pursuit of their goals. Such commoning institutions are highly virtuous from an ecological perspective, because they avoid waste in consumption and exploitation. Most important, commoning not only cares for the existing commons but also generates new social commons because people when doing things together exchange ideas and opportunities. Commoning generates the collective knowledge we need to solve today's systemic problems. Commoning within an ethical community is a choice, a shared individual decision stemming from the recognition that either we engage in an ecologically compatible lifestyle or we are living off our fellow commoners—those who are alive, those who are not yet born, and those that belong to a different species.[7]

REGENERATING THE COMMONS

Physical and virtual common spaces have been annihilated through individualistic logic and the legal institutions of capital. Extractive property institutions are responsible for this state of affairs. As a physical example, through property law, U.S. and other global northern companies collect the money of rich retirees investing in "time sharing," with which they corrupt cash-strapped local authorities in the global south to allow them to build ugly, polluting condominiums on the most beautiful coasts in the world, which should be safeguarded as a common. To run such time-share condominiums, locals are exploited beyond imagination and humiliated to solace the rich tourists.[8] As a virtual example, social bonds between the generations have been weakened because of the availability of cheap technology and lack of community ties. Children believe they have nothing to learn from previous generations, whose accumulated knowledge seems to be easily available on a tablet.[9]

To avoid such social and ecological disasters, the commons cry out to be recognized and protected by ecolaw. Supporting the regeneration of power-sharing institutions that have been devastated by capitalism and avoiding the lethal consequences of hundreds of years of violation of the principles of ecology—the actual "laws of nature"—will require a global, radical modification of extractive human laws. But how can such a massive task be accomplished?

We might begin by looking at how scientists approach lakes and sea basins affected by eutrophication—excessive plant growth stimulated by high nutrient concentrations. A well-known example is the inordinate growth of algae—which feeds on phosphates and nitrates left over from intensive chemical agriculture—which can disrupt the ecological balance of a body of water (for example, a lake) by distorting the system's feedback loops in ways that make it impossible for the ecosystem to regenerate.

One approach to this problem is to identify the corrupting element and its role in triggering a chain of negative ecological results. Ecologists then proceed to insulate some areas of the lake from the corruptive element, giving natural processes time to repair themselves. Once a small area is nursed back to health, the area of renewed healthy networks may be progressively extended until eventually the whole lake has recovered. Exceptional results can be reached by this kind of incremental ecological procedure, which can be implemented by law.

Using a similar ecological cure, we would consider the extractive legal institutions of modernity—state sovereignty and private ownership—as "algal blooms" of human laws, or as Nile perches in Lake Victoria. Ecoliteracy among jurists and the general public enables us to identify the problem and its effects, while ecodesign, based on a wealth of experience from the past as well as in the present, will inform our proposed remedies, which must be experienced in diffused practice and political experimentation.

A body of water is not regenerated all at once, and ecolaw likewise must work in stages, regenerating the global system incrementally, by attempting a variety of institutional solutions from the bottom up and making different alliances with the public or the private sector as needed. For instance, in certain circumstances it might be advisable to try to turn a common such as a beautiful beach into a trust, which is a private-property institution, in order to obtain the guarantees of due process of law that might protect it against corrupt government privatization. In other cases, such as the water companies of Paris or Naples, our final examples in the next chapter, it might be useful to turn them into a public ownership structure, to avoid the easy transfer of stocks to private investors.

Therefore, in taking this approach, we do not need to worry about the shortcomings of international law, which is itself an extractive setting in need of progressive regeneration and conversion, because while we think globally, we act locally, where physical and cultural resistance can happen. Nor do we need to tackle all the limits of the national political process that make a fix look impossible. Instead, we must work one person at a time, developing a new common understanding among an ecologically and legally literate population that is aware of both the laws of nature and the nature of law. Such a population, struggling to create its own common institutions and to protect them against the predatory spirit of both the private and the public sectors, is the fundamental ingredient of a commons-based recovery.

Regenerating the commons, challenging capitalist accumulation, reshaping the law from the bottom up, and eventually changing the whole of our common understanding requires a robust theory and the daily widespread political resolve of individuals. They must claim an active role that produces the empowerment of relationship. Successful contemporary and historical best legal practices, capable of implementing the values of power diffusion, social justice, and ecological sustainability wherever they are located, should be discussed, understood, adapted to different circumstances, and applied so that the voices, interests, and legal ways of these communities can once again prevail. It is worth restating: the variety of human experience is complex, but the fundamental organizational principle of commoning everywhere is that of caring, duty, reciprocity, and participation.

THE EXAMPLE OF THE TEATRO VALLE COMMONS FOUNDATION

Even a sophisticated arts institution can be run as a common. In Rome, the beautiful and antique Teatro Valle, a jewel of early eighteenth-century architecture, was occupied by a crowd of artists and entertainment industry workers reacting against a privatization project. Since the theater was declared a common in June 2011, it has offered hundreds of hours of cultural, political, and artistic entertainment, on a needs-based basis, outside of the recognition of any state law. Artists, sometimes of high national and international standing, have performed without a profit motive, and the occupiers have kept the place open, functioning, and clean. The Valle common, despite much controversy about its formal illegality, has worked in a fully open, consent-based, participatory fashion for more than three years.[10]

Following on this success, the occupants have organized themselves, within an alternative model of legality, as a "commons foundation" that has been endowed with €250,000 in cash and art collected during the first two years of occupation. The commons foundation is functionally a trust in the interest of culture and of future generations, with a membership of about six thousand, a permanent assembly known as the commune (*la comune*), and a rotating steering committee. No majority vote is taken, but decisions require consensus to be reached, taking all the time necessary. Participation requires that no one is left out of the important decisions, leaving each occupant much freedom to express his or her personality.

The foundation thus has become the venue and facilitator of the most advanced experiment in alternatives to the current public-private divide in property law. This experience has proved highly generative of arts and culture, and it has inspired similar experiments in theaters and other occupied spaces in other Italian cities, which are now connected into an organized network of support in a struggle for culture as a common. It has also attracted international attention: in Brussels in 2013, the European Cultural Foundation granted the prestigious Princess Margriet Award to the Valle.

As with its ecological counterpart, this remedy to the "algal bloom" of human laws continues to spread outward. Beginning with the Valle, this constituent effort to create a legal system of the commons, legitimized by actual struggles from the bottom up, became an itinerant group of jurists who meet in venues of ecologically devastating practices. These have included a mega-tunnel through the Alps (the Susa Valley), a bridge to Sicily, giant cruise ships entering the Venetian lagoon, offshore oil exploration projects, toxic-waste disposal in Naples, and many others. Similar experiences—from helping students to resist unfair loans as a follow-up to Occupy Wall Street, to the already mentioned work of Podemos in Spain to protect against foreclosures—are beginning to provide an important popular perception of the actual working of the law.

The most important aspect of these efforts is not merely obtaining some judicial victory that might generate some friendly case-law. Rather, it is to create a legal literacy diffused across the protagonists of the commons struggles for the full understanding of the nature of law in a genuine democracy and the possibility of transforming it through resistance against violations of the most basic laws of nature. Starting from such experiences, and the many others documented in the international literature,[11] one can outline what an ecological legal order *could* be, if the different commoning practices were to connect with one another, thus gaining strength and perspective. This exercise in imagination, well grounded in some actual practices, might become highly valuable as a theoretical approach to legal issues that social communities must face in creating the ecological legal order, and it might inspire others who seek fundamental change.

Despite movements such as Teatro Valle, the commons today lack adequate legal recognition in Western legal systems because of the structural imbalance that favors private interests over the public good.

Today capital has its favorite legal structure in the for-profit stock corporation, a perpetual machine of accumulation. An appropriate legal form for the commons has not yet been well developed, though a variety of trust structures could be, and sometimes are, deployed to defend such interests. Legal recognition that allows the commons to enjoy the same protection as private ownership and the same legitimacy as state sovereignty is a prerequisite for the development of an ecolegal order, and commoners—those who struggle for the commons—must be ready to organize themselves in legal form. The Foundation Teatro Valle offers a very interesting model to explore.

THE EMERGENCE OF ECOLAW FROM SELF-ORGANIZING COMMUNITIES

A legal regime capable of asserting control over our runaway system of exploitation needs to arise from self-organizing community action, such as that of the Valle occupants, based on ecoliteracy, ecodesign, and a legal consciousness for the protection of the commons. This action must be not just local but also must connect globally. A global, top-down, eco-friendly enforcement system at this point is impossible to conceive of. It would be ineffective because powerful policy makers and their allied corporate lawyers have global jurisdiction and are bound to uphold the existing system. Consequently, seeking the use of "top down" international law to protect the commons is like trying to employ a fox to protect a chicken house.

An ecolegal order would recognize the fundamental interconnectedness of our global problems and enable us to find appropriate, mutually supportive solutions that, instead of distinguishing law, politics, and economics at the local, state, or even international level, would mirror the interdependence of the problems they address. Systemic solutions typically solve several problems at the same time. For example, changing from our chemical, large-scale, energy-intensive, industrial agriculture to organic, community-oriented, sustainable farming would dramatically reduce our energy dependence, because (in the United States) we are now using one-fifth of our fossil fuels to grow and process food. Such a shift would have a huge positive effect on public health, because many chronic diseases are linked to our diet. And this shift would contribute significantly to fighting climate change, because an organic soil is a carbon-rich soil, which means that it draws CO_2 from the atmosphere and locks it up in organic matter.[12]

We have the knowledge, the technologies, and the financial means to build a sustainable future. What we need now is the capacity to transform the systemic vision into radically new human laws, capable of creating the correct incentive scheme to move in a safe direction. Such laws are most likely to emerge from self-organizing communities created, piece by piece, from the bottom up. This process will eventually change the default rules of the current social system so that the law, even in the absence of struggles that introduce some exceptions to its extractive logic, would favor the commons as a matter of default, just as today it favors the corporation.

LAW ITSELF AS A COMMON

Making the law part of the solution to our problems requires us to imagine an ecodesign approach to law. We need a small-scale, bottom-up approach whose effectiveness lies in its widespread use and its coherence with the needs and perceptions of communities at large. We need to begin to look at law itself as a common, which requires lawyering in strict symbiosis with community to fight the extractive legal order. Such community lawyering, to be generative, must include practicing the reciprocal education of lawyers and commoners to help each other in reaching an ecolegal understanding. This includes direct participation of community members in preparing the materials for litigation, and educating legal professionals in becoming commoners of the law; such a combination offers economically accessible services of high ecolegal value. In the Susa Valley "No-TAV" struggle, a landmark of the Italian struggles for the commons, a legal team of such a kind was put in place with reciprocal community and professional satisfaction.

Implementing such a legal approach first requires an understanding that, in the real life of the law, legitimacy does not stem just from a political process. Instead, the most important source of law is the laboratory of the real-life experience. The shared uses and values of a community, functional for a given social activity, over time are institutionalized as customs or binding practices. Sometimes known as social norms, these rules enjoy a degree of legitimacy that is much older than the birth of the modern state.

Indeed, such customary law has been the basis of the development of commercial law from antiquity and the Middle Ages to our time. Merchants have traditionally engaged in commerce on a broader scale than the jurisdictional borders of political authority. Dealers from Carthage would sell their products in different places in the Mediterranean, competing with the Romans. Arab merchants would sail all the way to the North Sea. Dutch, Portuguese, and Venetian boats would reach faraway marketplaces. In dealing with each other, these merchants were very informal. Often a handshake would be sufficient to cement an agreement, because these repeated dealings were based on reputation.[13]

Over time a complex system of customary mercantile law emerged from these handshakes, establishing standards of good behavior and generating progressively more complex transnational customary law, known as *lex mercatoria*. The top-down intervention of the progressively stronger and centralized states on these business customs and self-enforcing law was always very limited; it is very limited even today, when the decisions of a system of private arbitration are recognized and enforced by most legal systems with no questions asked.[14] Without doubt, this spontaneous legal order is legitimate and respected by the economic actors involved, even in the absence of state enforcement. In other words, legitimacy stems from decentralization, from the consensual way in which individuals and groups relate to one another. Interestingly, mercantile law emerged as a separate and legitimate system because merchants were legally literate about their practices, so that they could understand and self-enforce their law very well through their guilds. For example, bankruptcy emerged and took its name from the custom of crashing the counter (*banco*) where the insolvent merchant would sell his stuff in the marketplace to signal that he was out of business.

Likewise, direct community participation is crucial to ecolaw and could be obtained by relatively simple institutional devices, such as popular juries to check investment decisions, monitor the social and environmental costs of production, or advocate for future generations and the planet as a whole. Democratic oversight of the economy is possible, interesting, fun, and indeed is well overdue. Such oversight would monitor what is produced, how it is produced, and for whom it is produced, guided by the twin values of ecological sustainability and social justice. Such a conversion of the economy is quite feasible, once individuals transform themselves from consumers to citizens. We might call this model "everybody's rule of law"—a system of effective control of individual economic activities to ensure ecological integrity and social justice.[15] Ecolaw is just such a legal system, capable of considering human laws as part of new laws on behalf of nature and nonhuman interests.

COMMONING AND THE NEW ECOLEGAL ORDER

Throughout these pages, we have emphasized that the commons must be the organizing principle of the new ecolegal order just as the ecological community is the building block of nature. Commoning, defined as participating as a community in caring for the public good, generates the collective knowledge we need to solve today's systemic problems. No hierarchical structure based on the concentration of power and exclusion can do that. For example, think of Wikipedia. No other encyclopedia could harvest so much collective intelligence and knowledge. The aggregate of many is smarter than one individual only, no matter how smart and knowledgeable such an individual might be. Unfortunately, the current dominant power structure makes such recognition of the wealth of the commons very difficult. This is why the critical vision stemming from the actual commoning of knowledge and experience outside of the dominant communication media is so crucial.

Capitalist media simply do not like to publicize the successes of noncapitalist alternatives. This quite rudimentary strategy of silencing is very useful in making citizens feel too disempowered to change. Though our global human civilization is now on the verge of crashing because of the persistent disregard of the principles of ecology, capitalism has organized for itself a chorus of pundits and academics who produce a narrative that transforms the people from a political entity into a crowd of lonely consumers, too fearful and busy to resist.[16] The remedy of slowing down global economic growth, though voiced by many, hardly reaches the dominant media discourse. Consequently, the official political process neither represents nor supports available viable solutions. Instead, both corporate media and governments proactively work against the recognition of the danger. The capacity of capitalism to normalize dissent and go back to shortsighted business as usual is just staggering. Property and sovereignty, fostering individual accumulation of wealth and power, defend their stake to the point of no return.[17]

Community is where recognition of this state of affairs can happen and where resistance for self-defense can be organized. Some people, especially in the United States, fear community and communitarianism because they perceive it as a threat to their freedom, or even as a danger of oppressive state communism. However, putting the commons at the center of ecolaw, in order to make it in tune with nature and community, does not require a return to closed medieval communitarianism, nor to some communist autocracy such as the one often portrayed by the American media. These fears ironically are rarely displayed in the face of corporate capitalism, which hides behind the fetishism of free individual choice.[18] The strengthening of communal ties is essential for developing a political organization capable of restoring the quality of human relationships, a network of collective purposes where sharing and inclusion prevails over individualism and the brutish profit motive.

True, commoners monitor each other, limiting exploitation and extraction. However, community is also the only condition in which individuals empower one another, share knowledge and understanding, and produce strategies of resistance against the bullying of capitalist institutions, both government and corporate.

Ecological communities, the model for ecolaw, are never closed. They depend on energy and nutrients from their environment, and on occasional disturbances for their evolution. Similarly, social communities in their different forms reinforce one another by entering networking relationships with other communities that share the same general living purpose.[19] Community can be giving, hospitable, and open to guests. It can also be selfish, closed, and bigoted. This is true also for flesh and blood individuals, while corporations are built to be selfish and shortsighted only.[20] Institutions of ecolaw need to make sure that the community, just like the individual, develops these former characteristics and not the latter. The community functioning at the core of ecolaw does not separate the social from the natural, because it understands the ideological separation between nature and culture as well as that between law, politics, and the economy. Likewise, the new ecolegal order must allow collective agency to emerge once more, reclaiming the law as a collective tool of political transformation. Such participatory decision making, both political and economic, is a crucial aspect of the need to put the legal system at the center of, not the individual physical or legal person, but the "whole"—communities, networks, qualitative dimensions of relationships, with direct access to and stewardship of knowledge, law, and resources.

A good example of such a scheme of economic democracy, in which one of us (Mattei) has been involved personally, is the transformation of a corporation owning the water supply system of Naples into a newly crafted institutional entity, *Acqua Bene Comune* (water as common good). The purpose of this transformation was to make the water system of Naples owned and managed by the people and the workers in the interest of the whole community and of future generations. This experiment was the outcome of a long struggle to protect public water against privatization in Italy, which included a national referendum in which 27 million Italians voted in favor of considering water to be a common.[21]

A similarly spirited institution, born as a reaction to preposterous practices that originated from a deal between two multinational corporations, Veolia and Suez, that split the water market of Paris in two, one for the *rive gauche* (left bank) and one for the *rive droite* (right bank) of the Seine River. A victorious candidate for mayor of Paris, who had campaigned for water as a common, not only re-publicized the water supply system but also developed an advanced system of governance based on stakeholder participation in the newly created *Eau de Paris* (water of Paris).

In a nutshell, both institutions start from the premise that the water supply system should be run not for profit but as a service to the community and as a guarantee to future generations. *Eau de Paris* and *Acqua Bene Comune Napoli* share a living ecological and social purpose that is written into their bylaws. Their boards of directors are bound by this purpose and banned from profit-making moves. Public participation is ensured. In traditional corporate logic, the success of the activity is quantitatively measured by the market's rate of profit. In the world of the commons, the market cannot be used as a measure of success, because here the logic of success, coherent with ecolaw, is qualitative. Instead of the market, success is measured by stakeholder participation in governance. Sharing collective responsibility gives the legitimate agency of collective control to both public and private economic activity. The control thus provided is qualitative and based on a hard-nosed collective effort, by workers, consumers, environmental activists, and a few elected city council members to understand and guide the management in a way coherent with the bylaws. The traditional corporate form, whether private or public, is designed to sell as much water as possible because, if water is like any other commodity sold in a monopolistic market, profits will increase with the quantity of the product that is sold. In contrast, if water is treated as a common, the main purpose is to save as much of it as possible by investing in community ecoliteracy and limiting all the wastes. The market is ill-equipped to monitor the reach of this living corporate purpose of saving water and reducing the sell.

We still have a long way to go in elaborating the appropriate legal structures to run water, transportation, waste disposal, and other public activities as commons, but the examples of Naples and Paris suggest that such attempts, while difficult, are not impossible to achieve.

THE ETHICS OF COMMUNITY

Putting the commons at the center of the legal landscape will affect some of our extractive freedoms, which, as we have seen, are currently founded on unlimited property rights and the rule of law. Given our current deteriorating ecological condition, however, it is fair to question the extent to which extractive freedoms should be protected. It is unfair to sacrifice the rights of the unborn and of the victims of climate change in the name of unlimited extraction.

Those unpersuaded by ecological reasons to give up self-serving practices and rhetoric might be persuaded by basic ethical reasons. We often see this, for example, in the discussion of eating meat. Meat eating used to be an exceptional thing, usually carried on in particular circumstances, and in many cultures it is associated with some sacred meaning.[22] Many cultures and religions also have legal rules about eating meat and ban its inordinate consumption. It is also increasingly clear that eating large amounts of meat is ecologically unsustainable because intensive breeding results in widespread ecological, social, and health effects throughout the food chain.

Today, however, far from limiting meat consumption, capitalism has commoditized meat eating, as it has other cultural and qualitative aspects of human experience, for the purpose of corporate profit. The law of free enterprise has transformed human beings into ruthless exterminators of sentient animals.[23] Some people become vegetarian for ethical reasons related to the idea that sentient and intelligent creatures are bred in appalling conditions and are subjected to incredible suffering just to satisfy our free dietary choice. Others do so out of environmental concerns, since the production of meat, especially beef, consumes huge amounts of natural resources—water and topsoil first and foremost—while emitting massive amounts of methane, a powerful greenhouse gas.

Most people, however, being disconnected from nature, consider meat as just another packaged food item and simply do not question this unsustainable habit. Would it be unconceivable to attempt a reduction of the pro-capita amount of meat that each individual consumes with strategies similar to those that are used for cigarettes or alcohol, graphically picturing the suffering inflicted?

Thus, an appeal to ethics might be a powerful way to make people care for the commons just as certain societies are successful in deploying ethics to have people use self-enforcement without any formally enacted law. Behaving in an ethical way always means behaving in a way that is appropriate to our community. There are dos and don'ts that arise from belonging to a family, a professional community, a nation, or a cultural tradition. Ecoliteracy tells us that we all belong to *oikos*, the "Earth household" (the Greek root of the word "ecology"), and therefore we must behave accordingly.

Ethical behavior within the Earth household means behavior that respects the basic principles of ecology and therefore contributes to sustaining the web of life. Commoning within an ethical community is a choice, a shared individual decision stemming from the recognition that either we engage in an ecologically compatible lifestyle or we are living off our fellow commoners—who are, it is worth repeating, those who are alive, those who are not yet born, and those that belong to a different species.

CHAPTER 10

The Ecolegal Revolution

The Scientific Revolution introduced the concept of nature as a machine and human reason as superior to natural processes. The subsequent Industrial Revolution produced great "progress" in terms of technological development and efficient production, and the institutional transformation of some commons into concentrated capital served a real social need to overcome a brutal subsistence way of life. Concentrated capital meant industry, scientific and artistic development, better medicine, and eventually more hygienic conditions for many.

However, capital concentration also required the "commodification" of land. Toward that end, the landed class allied with government institutions to defeat the resistance of people who were living communally with subsistence agriculture and limited specialization. Their traditional productive processes were transformed into modern capitalist food production and manufacturing. This effort was aided by a theory of unlimited property rights, based on an ideology of freedom, improvement, and productive labor, which John Locke provided, and by a theory of unlimited state sovereignty, offered by Thomas Hobbes.[1]

THE SHADOW SIDE OF "PROGRESS"

The current dominant legal order serves the needs of capital accumulation. To do so, it has progressively separated itself from politics and the economy, the domains where the law can serve human needs. In the political domain, with the progressive extension of suffrage, the modern legal order has taken the form of liberal constitutionalism, which governs the world today. In the economic domain, it has taken the form of a laissez-faire market capitalism that only the state can limit. As we discussed in Chapter 6, the current Western vision of social institutions artificially separates individuals from one another and from their ecosystems. The two simple theories of property (Locke) and sovereignty (Hobbes) are ideologically presented as in opposition to each other, but these theories are actually coherent in their structure (concentration and individualization of power, and exclusion) and purpose (transformation of commons into capital).

The deal between these theories has incrementally destroyed the communal institutions that once provided subsistence and that were coherent with the reproductive requirements of nature. Yet the narrative of growth, innovation, modernization, and improvement has convinced even the losers in these social processes that wealth is measured only through money, exchange value, and accumulation, putting aside any nonmonetary human values. People have been persuaded that it is worthwhile to work hard, selling time for wages in order to participate in the process of accumulation and consumption. In this conception, for instance, domestic work such as caring for children or the elderly, or producing one's own food, clothing, or shelter does not count as production, does not produce wealth, and does not contribute to gross domestic product because it occurs outside of a market exchange. Likewise, the only recognized way to satisfy wants is to purchase goods and services on the market.

Since the time of the enclosure movement, relentless propaganda around the triumphs of the scientific and technological revolution has made country dwellers (who are often described with offensive terms) internalize the idea that their lifestyle is primitive, brutal, lacking culture, and inferior to life in the city. For most urban dwellers, urban life ultimately comprises long hours in unhealthy factories, hours of stressful commuting, or low-wage employment without benefits or security. Masses in the countryside believe they lack any culture, despite being the only members of society who would still be able to do something as crucial as generating food in an ecologically sustainable manner, using their mastery of very antique and sophisticated collective knowledge.

The result of such an ideology is that today this ancient collective knowledge is dying out; it is being replaced by industrial products, and thus the very means of survival is being outsourced to a small number of global corporations. Increased use of technology in agriculture has made food production water- and petroleum-intensive, transformed country life to an industrial mode of production (increasingly independent from ecological cycles), and made us believe that knowledge, like technology, is cumulative. We tend to believe that we always know more than before, just as each generation of cellular phones is a progression from the previous one, while in fact we are losing enormous amounts of local knowledge about natural processes. Today many farmers only know how to transform petroleum into industrial food with the use of chemicals, GMOs, and heavy machinery. Very few know local plants, medicinal or otherwise, the processes of hybridizing seeds, or the use of locally specific natural systems to limit the impact of pests.

In modern Western societies, this ideological construction (which becomes a self-fulfilling prophecy) continues to prove difficult to resist. In the 1950s and 1960s, for instance, many Italian girls would not marry men who were unwilling to seek jobs in northern factories. Others became ashamed of making their own pasta, feeling it was a sign of poverty, and would go out of their way to purchase industrially produced pasta. Large-scale, Marshall Plan–funded projects for energy extraction or industry, which devastated the beautiful coast of southern Mediterranean countries, were coveted by multitudes craving an industrial job and economic progress. Videos of ancient olive trees being eradicated by huge tractors were shown on TV, celebrating the might of progress and dubbing the smell of pollution as "the scent of modernity" and the previous lifestyle as "the archaic economy of the olive."[2]

In Italy, beautiful mountain villages, with incredibly sophisticated, collectively produced and maintained water supply systems and centuries-old homes of stone and wood, have been abandoned by residents seeking industrial employment. Today no one goes to a cobbler anymore. Corporations have increasingly concentrated oligopolies on ownership and delivery of water, fuel, seeds, and other necessities. Few people know how to build even a simple structure such as a shed, and most of us would look dreadful if we made our own clothing. In the dominant rhetoric, "the market" frees us from those chores by means of the efficient division of labor. However, choosing to use the market requires having enough money to do so. An individual who is bound to use the market is actually less free if there is no alternative. Consider, for example, an individual living in a U.S. city where it is very difficult to buy fresh vegetables, public childcare is very expensive, and her income is insufficient. In such a situation, possibly the nonmarket value of the self-production of food, clothing, and childcare would be higher than a paycheck at Walmart. As a massively urbanized society, we are hooked on market mechanisms making only cheap McDonald's hamburgers—heavily subsidized by the environment and by public health—affordable to many.

The shadow side of our attempt to dominate and exploit nature has now become all too evident. The harmonious forms of premodern architecture and the beauty and uniqueness of artisanal products, all based on centuries of transmitted knowledge, have been replaced by plastic, industrially produced, environmentally subsidized artifacts. How long does an IKEA closet last, compared to the ones built by our artisans? Is it really cheaper if we take into account its life span and the amount of natural and human exploitation that it entails, including the number of artisans who are put out of business by this industrial mode of production? In fact, it is not cheaper, either socially or from the individual point of view. However, the 99 percent in industrialized countries cannot afford quality and the 1 percent can *freely choose* to make bigger profits on environmentally subsidized artifacts with a short life span.

Most artisanal and farming skills have been lost through the conscious effort to make every individual dependent upon large-scale industrial production. This production, in turn, requires tremendous capital concentration, which then requires more appropriation of the commons, in an increasingly destructive cycle.

The transformation of territory from a place of life and relationship with fellow humans and nature into a commoditized land available for "development" has resulted in a dead, monocultural landscape of gas stations and shopping malls. Moreover, this institutional deal and its supporting ideology have come to seem like "common sense." Who today can envision a different kind of economy or social order? In a very short amount of time, generative institutions based on long-term collective relationships have been dismissed from the official legal order and are not an object of public conversation.

Constructing laws for exclusion and the concentration of power was the key to transforming both the physical and the cultural commons into private property and capital that are concentrated in a few powerful private or public hands. Today, however, the world is vastly different from the one on which Locke, Hobbes, Hugo Grotius, Jean Domat, Blackstone, and Adam Smith were reflecting. They lived in a world with plenty of commons and very little capital, but today we have plenty of capital and virtually no remaining commons. Nonetheless, we continue to employ the same extractive institutions that have so successfully created this state of affairs in a little more than three hundred years. Our urgent need now is to transform our tremendous capital surplus into commons, and we simply cannot do that by applying the old extractive logic of quantitative growth.

The mechanistic institutional system embodies a clash between the linear thinking and production processes of capitalism and the nonlinear patterns in the biosphere—the ecological networks and cycles that constitute the web of life.[3] Whereas this highly nonlinear, natural global network contains countless feedback loops through which the planet balances and regulates itself, our current economic system is fueled by materialism and a legal structure that do not recognize any limit, and it is supported by legal ideas such as the individual freedom to accumulate property.

In Chapter 3, we mentioned the crude amount of violence deployed to impose the pincer of property rights and sovereignty during the early phase of the accumulation of capital through enclosures and colonization. The peasant insurrections and wars that characterized the fifteenth and sixteenth centuries were repressed with both violence and ideology. For example, Martin Luther fiercely condemned the participants of revolts and openly justified killing them, dubbing them "dogs with rabies."[4] Today, the resistance of people who are increasingly aware of the false consciousness of the dominant narrative is quashed with a corresponding physical and ideological strategy. In Western countries, activists are increasingly prosecuted under terrorism charges. Embattled European governments are following the lead of England and the United States in introducing progressively harsher laws and repressing protests by arrests and criminal prosecution.

In France a young boy who was demonstrating against the construction of a dam was killed in November 2014 by increasingly militarized police forces.[5] The violence of law, which is mostly targeted toward disempowered minorities, is appalling. Institutions should have a purpose. While the task of the military is to deal with an enemy, in a democracy the task of the police should be to protect the citizens. The confusion of these roles in dealing with the ecological activism of those who struggle for a different world is indeed a grim sign of our times.

However, when oppression leads to catastrophe, and when a system can only justify itself through violence, conditions for revolution quickly develop.

ECOLITERACY—THE CONCEPTUAL FOUNDATION OF THE ECOLEGAL REVOLUTION

Because we humans have only one planet, our ecological footprint should be equal to one planet—that is, we should consume only a fraction of our common wealth, enabling anyone else in the world to do the same, while maintaining conditions suitable to sustaining and reproducing life.[6] Today, however, our global ecological footprint is 1.5 planets, which means that we would need one and a half planets to sustain our global lifestyle. Sometime in August each year we begin living off of resources that cannot be reproduced, thus accelerating the approaching point of no return. In fact, the footprint is 1.5 only because many people in the world live far below the standard of one planet, due to material poverty. Currently, the footprint of North Americans is almost five planets, and that of Europeans is more than three planets. Were everyone in the world to live like those in the United States, the "land of the free," we would need five planets to survive!

Earlier in history, people might have been ignorant of this trend; they were unable to see the big picture and pursued goals much different from ours, in a much different world. Today, however, knowledge of nature's inherent processes and patterns of organization is no longer confined to academic ecologists and philosophers. It is now quite clear that understanding the basic principles of ecology and living accordingly is critical for our survival on the planet. It is equally clear that capitalism resists a transformation that necessarily requires more sharing and less consuming, a condition that can happily happen only within communities of shared ideals. Designing such a new world requires nothing less than a cultural revolution capable of transforming the culture of the extractive individual toward that of a generative community. We must be ready to do so.

The shared goal of our time should be to use human laws in tune with nature to build and nurture sustainable communities—social, cultural, and physical environments in which we can satisfy our needs and aspirations without diminishing the chances of future generations. There are many differences between ecosystems and human communities. For example, an ecosystem has no self-awareness. It also has no language, no consciousness, and no culture, and therefore no justice or democracy—but also no greed or dishonesty. The wisdom of nature must become a central part of human law, but human laws are rules of conduct for a community, and their central concern is with human values. Thus, we cannot learn anything about human values and shortcomings from ecosystems, nor is it enough to say that we must mimic ecology. But we can and must learn from ecosystems how to live sustainably, which requires us to make our diverse human values consistent with the fundamental value of sustaining life on Earth.

It is worth repeating: what is sustained in a sustainable community is not economic growth or competitive advantage but the entire web of life on which our long-term survival depends. In other words, a sustainable community is designed in such a way that its ways of life, businesses, economy, physical structures, and technologies do not interfere with nature's inherent ability to sustain life but instead facilitate its generative force. This transformation requires giving up some of the cult of individualistic freedom that became dominant with the Enlightenment, a consequence of humanism being co-opted by capital.

We urgently need to redesign our human laws, both as external constraints and as an internal transformation of the current institutional DNA of governments and corporations. As much as possible of the tremendous amount of capital accumulated by extraction needs to be put back into commons. To transform the laws, we must transform ourselves in such a way that we can understand their nature, and the tremendous power that we have as a community over the law. We must be aware that laws exist so long as they are obeyed, and that we make them in the choice we pursue as a community between obedience and disobedience. Just as the choice of disobedience by Rosa Parks was necessary to change the status of segregation from legal to illegal, similar resistance is needed to change extractive laws and practices from legal to illegal.[7]

The first step on the road toward sustainability, naturally, must be to understand how nature sustains life. This involves a new ecological understanding of life as well as the new kind of systemic thinking that we have been discussing. For billions of years, the Earth's ecosystems have evolved certain principles of organization to sustain the web of life. These principles of organization, or principles of ecology, are today's equivalent of what used to be called the laws of nature. They are perhaps more subtle, and they are formulated in qualitative ways—in terms of patterns of relationships and of processes—but they are as stringent as Newton's law of gravity.

Knowledge of these principles of ecology is known as ecological literacy, or ecoliteracy.[8] In the coming decades the survival of humanity will depend on our ecoliteracy and our ability to live accordingly. Hence, ecoliteracy must become a critical skill for politicians, business leaders, and professionals in all spheres, especially in jurisprudence, and should be the most important part of education at all levels, including the continuing education and training of professionals. Our children, our students, and our political and corporate leaders must understand the fundamental facts of life: for example, that the waste of one species is food for another species; that matter cycles continually through the web of life; that the energy driving the ecological cycles flows from the sun; that diversity ensures resilience; that life did not take over the planet through combat but by networking.

All the principles of ecology are closely interrelated, different aspects of a single fundamental pattern of organization that has worked to create and nurture communities through billions of years of evolution. No individual organism can exist in isolation. Animals depend on the photosynthesis of plants for their energy needs; plants depend on the carbon dioxide produced by animals as well as on the nitrogen fixed by bacteria at their roots; and together, plants, animals, and microorganisms regulate the entire biosphere and maintain the conditions conducive to life.

This, then, is the profound lesson we need to learn from nature: sustainability is not an individual property but a property of an entire web of relationships, and it always involves a whole community. A sustainable human community interacts with other communities—human and nonhuman—in ways that enable each to live and develop according to their nature. Sustainability does not mean that things do not change. It is a dynamic process of coevolution rather than a static state.

To be sure, deeply held legal and scientific beliefs, especially those that are strongly supported by the dominant industrial culture, die hard because they have conquered the minds of people who in large part behave accordingly, without seriously questioning the status quo either out of fear or because the system seems to work for them personally. It takes a generation-long process to change commonly held beliefs; and this is where education is critical. Teaching ecoliteracy in schools today means ecoliterate students in law schools tomorrow, and eventually ecoliterate legal professionals in many positions of power throughout society.

ECODESIGN—LEARNING FROM THE WISDOM OF NATURE

After becoming ecoliterate, the next step on the roadmap to the ecolegal revolution is ecological design, or ecodesign—the radical redesign of our technologies and social institutions in order to bridge the current gap between human design and the sustainable systems of nature. From an ecological point of view, design is the shaping of flows of energy and matter for human purposes. Ecodesign, in the words of David Orr, "is the careful meshing of our human purposes with the larger patterns and flows of the natural world."[9] Ecodesign principles reflect the principles of organization that nature has evolved to sustain the web of life, nurturing a sense of community rather than separating people from nature and rendering them ecologically illiterate. The practice of such design requires a fundamental shift in our attitude toward nature, from finding out, as ecodesigner Janine Benyus puts it, "not . . . what we can *extract* from nature, but . . . what we can *learn* from her."[10]

In recent years, there has been a dramatic rise in ecologically oriented design practices and projects.[11] For example, we are seeing a worldwide renaissance in organic farming where farmers use technologies based on ecological knowledge rather than chemistry or genetic engineering to increase yields, control pests, and build soil fertility. We are seeing the organization of different industries into ecological clusters, in which the waste of any one organization is a resource for another. Ecodesigners advocate the shift from a product-oriented economy to a "service-and-flow" economy, in which industrial raw materials and technical components cycle continually between manufacturers and users. Green architecture is a thriving field. We now have buildings that are designed to produce more energy than they use, emit no waste, and monitor their own performance. In transportation, we have hybrid-electric cars achieving fuel efficiencies two to three times that of standard cars; and the development of efficient hydrogen fuel cells promises to inaugurate a new era in energy production.

These ecodesign technologies and projects all incorporate the basic principles of ecology and therefore have some key characteristics in common. They tend to be small-scale projects with plenty of diversity, energy efficient, nonpolluting, community oriented, and labor intensive, creating plenty of jobs.

ECOLAW NOW!

Today we have the knowledge, the technologies, and the financial means to transform capital into commons. However, human laws, serving the imperatives of capitalist production, point us in the opposite direction. What we need, then, is political courage and leadership at all levels of society to challenge the unsustainable status quo. The legal dimension of this political will is highly important and requires a deep transformation of our understanding of what the law is. It requires the development of some ecologically oriented legal principles that can begin to translate the ecological worldview into institutional theory and practice. These principles can guide communities in deciding whether to obey the current law or whether to exercise the right of resistance in the interest of their own survival and of future generations, while avoiding disorder and individualistic behaviors, no matter how well intentioned.

We need a new narrative to make ecological behavior appealing, and a new legal system, created by widespread community resistance and networking. A legal system based on principles that are the polar opposite of the careless extractive transformation of commons into capital that we have celebrated over the past three hundred years. At the center of this narrative must be a shift from quantity to quality, and the wisdom, learned from nature, that well-being does not depend on consuming more than is necessary.

Translated into social categories, this means that freedom is a condition of being that is enjoyed in relationships, and has nothing to do with accumulating property—in spite of the masterful ideological construction of Locke.

The opposite to the current status quo of capitalist extraction requires an emphasis on social generation and reproduction, which produces values such as selflessness and cooperation, rather than individualistic self-assertion and competition. Commoning—spending time together to care for something recognized as a common with high attention and patience—makes life more meaningful and fun than struggling and getting stressed in accumulating power against someone else. There is plenty of occasion for everybody to flourish in horizontal communities within an economy of "enough" and not of "more."

We must, when possible, rediscover and admire the self-production of food, artifacts, and clothing. This does not mean, of course, that there should be no division of labor in the future. But we need to acknowledge that those of us who are capable of self-production are free from market dependency. It is important to understand that the star system and the cult of tycoons is an ideological construction to make the greedy ones—who eat much more than their fair share at the buffet of life—into respectable members of society rather than undesirable company.

A sustainable human future requires a significant amount of critical thinking and a jurisprudence conceptually founded on ecoliteracy. An ecological design of law will not be abstract and top-down but rather stem from the concrete needs of everybody and the different commoning experiences that are already active. Such an ecolegal order, produced by ecoliterate people, is capable of developing practical principles opposite to those that have transformed most of our commons into capital; thus it is capable of transforming a progressively increasing amount of our capital back into commons. This order must foster a diffusion of power and participatory democracy rather than a concentration of power and secrecy; inclusion, distributive justice, and sharing rather than exclusion, inequality, and selfishness.

In such a system, jurists would translate current ecological knowledge—learned from participation in social struggles, but also from conservation ecology, climate science, human ecology, and other related scientific fields—into policy and normative interpretations of the law. The ecological community, not the individual human being, must be at the core of ecolaw, because the most important "law of nature" is that the whole is not the simple aggregate of its parts.

To accomplish this, we must stop perceiving the law as a closed system of professionally drafted rules, organized around some principle of political sovereignty. Such a vision not only is far too narrow and doctrinal but also is based on the same pattern of exclusion and concentration of power that ecological thinking struggles against. In the dominant vision, people are excluded from the law by professional lawyers. Power is concentrated in the hands of professional groups that have been able, historically, to claim the social usefulness and indispensable nature of their initiated knowledge. In the Western legal tradition, as we have discussed in the previous chapters of this book, lawyers are one of the most important of such groups. Just as scribes in ancient Egypt were the only ones capable of keeping account of the quantity of cereals stored by the centralized institutions of government, so lawyers and scientists share a knowledge-based power strategy. Lawyers currently use this strategy to claim a monopoly on the knowledge of a legal system that is "out there" in cases and codes of law.

Ecoliterate people, aware of the necessity for change, should not accept the current power-based exclusion from the law. Like all commons, such as language or culture, the law belongs to its users. Legal knowledge should consequently be shared and diffused in order to profit from collective intelligence. This does not mean that there is no space for legal professionalism in the making of ecolaw. It only means that legal knowledge must be part of the collective effort to redesign society, providing generative legal institutions to replace the extractive ones that have dominated over the past quarter-millennium.

Such a daunting collective effort can only be successful if different kinds of knowledge and culture open up, giving up a practice of exclusion that is intimately connected with the state of affairs we need to change. Indeed, legal scholars have been broadening the perspective on their discipline for quite some time. Many studies in fields like legal anthropology, comparative law, law and society, and legal history have been objecting to the narrow vision of the legal system as strictly objective and immutable. All these disciplines have emphasized that law exists within a legal culture, both professional and popular, sometimes dubbed a "vernacular," that determines and affects the official making of laws.

However, many dominant approaches in our global legal institutions, such as the economic analysis of law or rational choice theory, have worked in the opposite direction. Their aim is to incrementally transform law into a mere technology, thus narrowing the picture and constructing it as an objective, universal artifact that is unable to respect local cultural variations. The ideological merger of the Newtonian vision of science with the narrow, objective vision of law as technology, all merging with mainstream economic theory to produce the illusion of perpetual growth and progress and an irrational faith in technology, is certainly a powerful ideology. But it is exactly this ideology, embedded in current institutional structures, that systems thinking and ecoliteracy reject and that we now need to overcome, both politically and culturally.

Regaining the sense of our collective ownership of the legal system—that is, approaching the legal system as a common—is a crucial part of the strategy to finally put human laws in tune with nature and community. The law is not a dead scheme of principles and rules written in books that only lawyers know how to read. Instead, it is present, an expression of our social, ethical behavior, made of obligations toward each other and toward the commons. If it is perceived as such by the whole community, it can once more become alive and generative. As such the law is an expression of the "whole"—something utterly different from the aggregate of its parts but produced by a relationship among the parts without exploitation and abuse.

ECOLEGAL PRACTICES

The Foundation Teatro Valle and the water companies of Naples and Paris, portrayed in the previous chapter, are examples of ecolegal practices based on participation. In Latin America important traits of ecolaw can be found in the constitutional rights granted to nature or to Pacha Mama from Ecuador to Bolivia to Venezuela.[12] These constitutions, broadly discussed in their making with communities in village assemblies and other participatory venues, have all ended up with the introduction of the notion of nature's rights, which the people, through state institutions and through collective practices of care, have a duty to protect. Like the corporation in North America, in certain countries of Latin America, nonhuman entities have thus been endowed with rights. Such constitutional declarations are perhaps more symbolic than effective at the moment, but they are nevertheless significant because they reflect and translate into written constitutional language the understanding of native people when they are allowed to participate. These very same communities for hundreds of years have lived collectively in nature with their mother Earth without knowledge of individualistic property rights.

Though it is still at a very infant stage, something is changing in the mentality of jurists, making some of them sensitive to nonhuman subjectivity, as recent transformations in Germany indicate. Again, the transformation has to do with property law. German property law has taken domestic animals off the list of "objects of property" in the Civil Code.[13] Other European legal systems have done so for wild animals, which can no longer be acquired by occupation because they are considered the property of the government. Scholars in the United States and elsewhere are working hard to elaborate forms of trust for future generations, to grant legal standing to trees, or even to establish an advocate for future generations, or a similar institutional device to protect commons that should be excluded from the logic of the market. Once more, fascinating examples are available from the past. The building of cathedrals was the collective effort of three, even four generations. In order to minimize the risk that authorities in office would discontinue the common effort, thus squandering resources, medieval notaries created legal institutions known as cathedral foundations, binding public property and resources to be maintained for that use; this practice was a sophisticated institution of the commons.

In a new ecolegal order, what today is the exception will become the rule. The generative DNA of each ecolegal person will be clearly spelled out in the bylaws of a commons institution, as has happened today in the water companies of Naples and Paris. Devices to encourage respect for the generative bylaws will be based on ecologically literate public participation, rather than on the market bottom line, as is the rule today. The market can successfully monitor the pursuit of the profit motive, but it is ill equipped to account for the ecological footprint of each institution. Reducing the catastrophic impact of exploitative activities and excessive economic growth, while accumulating ecological integrity and social justice, requires using community knowledge in order to preventively control the economic projects and practices that can endanger the future through a variety of sophisticated participatory institutions, which happens today only as an exception.

Business as usual is not possible anymore. Should car companies have the right to produce any kind of SUV, no matter how unreasonably big they are, for urban use? Should the top 1 percent avail itself of the unrestricted freedom to fly on private aircrafts just because they can afford it? Should these kinds of aircrafts be produced to begin with? Should companies be able to maintain intensive cattle breeding now that we know the devastating impact of excessive meat consumption? Should a fishing vessel be allowed to fish for any kind of fish, independently from the seasons? Should impoverished governments be allowed to sell beautiful Mediterranean isles to tycoons, excluding everyone else from them, as recently happened for Poveglia or Budelli Islands?

True, even the current conception of the law allows the exceptional introduction of environmental regulation to limit proprietary decisions. Ecolaw, however, by putting commons at the center, simply changes the exception into the rule. Ecologically literate lawyers, politicians, and people will find it completely reasonable to invert the relationship between the rule and the exception; the burden to prove the social acceptability of a given property scheme will be reversed. No commoner perceives the limit on the use of private aircraft as a limitation on the property freedom of the 1 percent. Rather, owning such an aircraft will be an unacceptable limitation on the freedom of the community to happily survive and reproduce itself on this planet. After all, when the United States was founded it was as natural to own slaves as today it is natural to fly a private jet if you can afford it.

Property will not be protected if it serves antisocial purposes, such as accumulating rent that results from public investment. Likewise, corporate entities will not be allowed to operate if they do not serve the community in which they reside. As we have mentioned, today's corporate structures allow corporations to form and to live forever, with their interests protected by property law founded on a mechanistic, extractive view. In many instances, most famously thus far in NAFTA (but in the making for the Trans-Pacific Partnership), property rights on extractive investment are protected by law against governments' attempts to protect the safety of the environment or the social standards guaranteed to workers in their territories.[14] Today, because of their power, corporations are able to buy eternal life for themselves. They can invest in creating a legal environment that is unfairly friendly to themselves, determine the results of electoral competitions for office, and outspend their opponents in litigation.

Ecolaw will not consider corporations, which are the current face of accumulated capital, as people, because unlike every other creature they are immortal.[15] In the United States, for example, the idea that economic interests can be incorporated no matter what their purpose is quite recent and dates back to the late nineteenth century. Before then the legal benefits of incorporation were granted only for specific purposes and were limited in time. Once the purpose of a corporation had been achieved, such as when the Charles River Bridge was completed, the corporation would dissolve, as naturally as individuals die. In ecolaw, the benefits of incorporation are restricted, with conditions to care for the environment and respect communities. Ecolaw will limit the scope, duration, and size of corporations, introducing such limits into their bylaws and organizing jury systems to check on whether these limits are being respected by the managers.[16]

Not only property and corporate law, but also contract law, at the very core of the legal system, will be modified in the ecological legal order. Legal contracts that are not coherent with long-term sustainability, such as many of the current project-financing deals to build mega-infrastructures, will be deemed illegal and not enforceable by courts of law. Freedom of contract, like the shield of limited liability for corporate investment, was one of the most powerful institutions developed by lawyers at the dawn of modernity to facilitate the transformation of commons into capital. In tort law, the fault system, letting the damages stay where they fall unless they are the outcome of "unreasonable" behavior, served the same function. Ecolaw will not be content with introducing some external exceptions to such principles but if necessary will change the very principles themselves to create general incentives to transform our current excessive capital back to the endangered commons.

Such modifications are crucial for tackling the current wrong-headed incentive structure inherited by a legal system designed for extractive rather than generative purposes. Institutional changes will also guarantee decisions in the interest of nature, a complex living network that cannot be served by the current legal structure, which only serves, at its best, living humans. In the ecological legal system someone will advocate for future generations and for the planet as a whole, just as today the attorney general advocates for the interest of the "state" or the corporate lawyer advocates for the "corporation." One tool for this purpose is broadening the rules for who has "standing to sue," a legal term meaning that an individual has sufficient stake in a controversy to obtain judicial resolution of that controversy. An attempt to introduce "diffused standing to sue" (that is, opening up the legal process disjunctively to everybody) as a rule in the protection of the commons was made in Italy by the Rodotà Commission in 2007. This commission, whose task was the reform of property law, has generated much of the Italian commons movement. Diffused standing to sue will fulfill our duty to grant animals, plants, and the not-yet-born access to ecological justice.[17] In the United States, the question of whether teenagers can sue governments for insufficient care of the environment in the interest of future generations has been litigated unsuccessfully for quite some time, but it now seems that at least a court in Oregon might be ready to make a crucial step in the direction of ecolaw.[18]

CONCLUSION: A VISION AND A PLAN

The current concentrated power structure will not concede any of these changes, which will ultimately decentralize power to small-scale communities in tune with the laws of ecology. Because structural changes do not happen by concession, the survival of civilization requires a revolution to move from a mechanistic, "pre-existing" law based on legal professionalism, capital, owners, and state sovereignty toward an ecology of law founded on social and natural relations and on community ownership. For such a revolution to happen, a dialogue between law and ecology is needed. Only the start of such a new dialogue can produce a coherent and clear way of thinking in the process.

In this book, we have indicated many alternative institutions that are already moving in this direction, working to create ecologically inspired communities, and based on an understanding of nature and community as networks rather than machines. Factories re-opened and re-converted by workers in the aftermath of crises; public spaces occupied and made available for production by artists; and co-ops of artisans and sustainable farming are among the examples. By looking at such efforts, we see the basic principles of ecolaw already in action and the traits of the law we want to reach.

We shall reach laws that serve the ecological community, rather than mimicking economic theory and serving the rational *homo oeconomicus* (or the "reasonable man," as lawyers like to say). Such a new ecological legal awareness—the genuine ecolegal revolution—will happen as soon as the 99 percent understand that they can take their laws into their own hands and, with them, their future.

As the great jurist Oliver Wendell Holmes famously said, "The life of the law has not been logic; it has been experience." If each struggle creates new institutional forms, if all practices of commoning learn from one another, and if commoners seize all possibilities of political impact according to the local political conditions, the ecolegal revolution will arrive sooner than expected. Ecology shows us that sometimes it takes a fire to regenerate a sick forest. The current legal system, which is institutionalizing extraction and devouring our future, is like rotten wood that is very difficult to set on fire. Any single strategy is likely to fail, as when one tries to light a fire with only one match. Many different attempts to light it, small as they might appear, will be successful, if all work together for a common and clear purpose of emancipation from the mechanistic vision of law. Insurgencies without a vision are just desperate riots—easy to delegitimize and to repress with the violence of current law. Ecolaw is ready *now* to endow the 99 percent with a vision and a plan.

Notes

INTRODUCTION

1. The most lively and well-known description of this state of affairs remains Perkins (2004).
2. See, e.g., Klein (2014).
3. See Meiksins Wood (2012).
4. See Capra and Luisi (2014).
5. This perspective is inspired by Nader (2005).
6. See Grossi (2010).
7. Ibid.
8. See Merchant (1990).
9. See Polanyi (1949).
10. See Foucault (1975).
11. See Meiksins Wood (2012), 267 ff.
12. See Hertz (2001).
13. For the best evidence of this statement in all its elegance and brilliance, see Robbins (1998).
14. See Galbraith (1958).
15. See http://www.nrdc.org /water/drinking/bw/chap2.asp.
16. For recent data on the ecological catastrophe, see Brown (2009).
17. For the tragedy of the commons, see Hardin (1968). The classic critique is Ostrom (1990).
18. See Dicker (2013).
19. See, in this sense, Hawken (2010).

CHAPTER 1. SCIENCE AND LAW

1. See Hart (2012).
2. See Pound (1910).
3. See Dawson (1983).
4. See Van Caenegem (1993).
5. See Dworkin (2013).
6. See Oakley (2005).
7. See Berman (1985).
8. See Plucknett (2001).
9. See Kuhn (1996).
10. See Barron et al. (2002).
11. See Dawson (1983).
12. See Twining (2009).
13. See Cardozo (1921) for the almost legendary "confession" of the creative role of the judiciary.
14. See Mattei and Nader (2008).
15. See Meadows (1972); Brown (1981); World Commission on Environment and Development (1987).

CHAPTER 2. FROM *KÓSMOS* TO MACHINE

1. See Capra (2007, 2013).
2. See Meiksins Wood (2012).
3. See Daston and Stolleis (2008).
4. Quoted in Rodis-Lewis (1978).
5. See Daston and Stolleis (2008).

CHAPTER 3. FROM COMMONS TO CAPITAL

1. See Grossi (2010).
2. See Lupoi (2006).
3. See Garnsey (2007).
4. See Watson (1995).
5. See Watson (1968).
6. See Honoré (1962).
7. See Buckland (1963).
8. See Wieacker (1995).
9. See Levy (1951).
10. See Buckland (1936).
11. See the masterful reconstruction of Linebaugh (2008).
12. See Marx ([1867] 1992). The theory of the so-called primitive accumulation is developed in vol. 1, part 8, chapter 26.
13. See Linebaugh (2008).
14. See Tigar (2005).
15. More ([1523] 2010), 10–11.
16. See Baker (2002).
17. See Foucault (1975).
18. The masterful and massive work of legal historian Paolo Grossi (2010) does justice to this state of affairs.
19. See Foucault (1975).
20. See Mattei (2011).
21. See Baker (2002).
22. See Milsom (1985).
23. See Merchant (1990).

24. See Gordley (1990).
25. Gordley (2013).
26. On the developments and transformations of academic legal theory in the Continent, see the recent thorough discussion in Gordley (2013).
27. See Meiksins Wood (2012), 119 ff.
28. See Haakonssen (1996).
29. See Mattei and Nader (2008).
30. See the classic Macpherson (1962).
31. See Cassi (2007).
32. See Grossi (2006).

CHAPTER 4. THE GREAT TRANSFORMATION AND THE LEGACY OF MODERNITY

1. See Mattei and Nader (2008).
2. Meiksins Wood (2012) especially stresses this point through her masterful work.
3. See Meiksins Wood (2012).
4. See Mattei and Nader (2008).
5. See Galeano (1973).
6. See Friedman (2010).
7. See Ellis (2002).
8. See Ely (2008).
9. See Blaug (1996).
10. See Lucarelli and Lunghini (2012).
11. Mofid and Szeghi (2010).
12. See Roy (2012).
13. See Hertz (2001).

CHAPTER 5. FROM THE MACHINE TO THE NETWORK

1. See Richards (2002); Berlin (2013).
2. See Eiseley (1961).
3. See Capra (1975).

4. Quoted in Capra (1975), 140.
5. See Capra (1996).
6. Maturana and Varela (1987); see also Capra (1996).
7. Prigogine and Stengers (1984); see also Capra (1996).
8. See Capra (2002).

CHAPTER 6. MECHANICAL JURISPRUDENCE

1. See Grossi (2010).
2. See Pound (2012).
3. See Swartz (1998).
4. See Stein (2009).
5. Hume ([1740] 2000), 490.
6. A similar method is famously deployed by Engels (1972).
7. See Whitman (1990).
8. See Levy (1951).
9. See Kennedy (2006).
10. A lively, very accessible discussion can be found in Gilmore (2014).
11. See Nader (2005).
12. See Gilmore (2014).
13. See Posner (2014).

CHAPTER 7. THE MECHANISTIC TRAP

1. See Siegle (2014).
2. See Kelly (2001); Stout (2012).
3. See Buchanan and Tullock (2004).
4. See Bollier (2014).
5. Regulation 1169/2011 on food information to customers was entered in application 13.12-2014. See http://ec.europa.eu /food/food/labellingnutrition /nutritionlabel/index_en.htm.
6. See Nader (2014).
7. See Noble (2013).

8. On the need for a total critique of this state of affairs, see Unger (1976).
9. See, e.g., Held and McGrew (2003).
10. See Hardt and Negri (2000).
11. See Castells (1996); Mander (2012); Mander and Goldsmith (1996); Piketty (2014).
12. See Klein (2007).
13. See Reimann (2013).
14. See Mallaby (2010).
15. See Mattei (2011).
16. See Castells (1998); Klein (2007).
17. *Eldred v. Ashcroft*, 538 U.S. 916 (2003); *Kelo v. City of New London*, 454 U.S. 469 (2005); *Kiobel v. Royal Dutch Petroleum*, 133 S. Ct. 1659 (2013); *American Express v. Italian Colors Restaurant*, 133 S. Ct. 594 (2013).
18. See Castells (1996).
19. See Kroft (2008).
20. See Kuttner (2010).
21. See Noble (2013).
22. See Ross (2013).
23. A list of these ideological arguments can be found in Dietze (1995).
24. See Gordley (2013).
25. See Unger (1976).
26. See Llewellyn (2012).
27. See Mattei (1997).
28. See Hertz (2001).

CHAPTER 8. FROM CAPITAL TO COMMONS

1. See Nader (2005).
2. Arendt (2006).

3. See Boyle (2003).
4. See Alford (1995).
5. On the role of "outlaws" in civilizing the legal system, see Penalver and Katyal (2010).
6. See Magnani (2009).
7. United Nations, "World's Population Increasingly Urban with More Than Half Living in Urban Areas," July 10, 2014, http://www.un.org /en/development/desa /news/population/world -urbanization-prospects -2014.html.
8. See World Nuclear Association, "Nuclear Power in Japan," http://www.world-nuclear .org/info/Country-Profiles /Countries-G-N/Japan/.
9. For a fundamental comparative study, see Valguarnera (2014).
10. See Harper (2012).
11. See Wildlife Society (2010).
12. See Zeller (2015).
13. For a variety of cases, see Gonzales and Philips (2014).
14. See the important recent book of Wrights (2014).
15. See Mattei (2000).
16. See Nader (1990).
17. See Hardt and Negri (2009).
18. See Grossi (1975).
19. See Collum et al. (2012).
20. For a superb collection of initiatives, see Bollier and Helfrich (2012).
21. Kelly (2012).
22. Ibid., 11.

CHAPTER 9. THE COMMONS AS A LEGAL INSTITUTION

1. For a recent and very accessible discussion, see Bollier (2014).
2. See Rodotà (2013).
3. For a discussion of the common as an institutional arrangement compatible with capitalism, see Barnes (2006).
4. See Riesman (2001).
5. See Tönnies (2001).
6. See Ostrom (1990).
7. For a brilliant real-life discussion, see Rowe (2013).
8. For a brilliant documentary, offering a systemic analysis of mass tourism, see Black (2001).
9. A thorough analysis of the social impact of market individualism can be found in Bauman (2001).
10. See Giardini, Mattei, and Spregelburd (2012).
11. See Bollier and Helfrich (2012).
12. See Paul Hepperly, "Organic Farming Sequesters Atmospheric Carbon and Nutrients in Soils," The Rodale Institute, http:// www.strauscom.com /rodale-whitepaper/.
13. See Grossi (2006).
14. See Dezalay and Garth (1998).
15. See Mattei and Nader (2008).
16. See Klein (2014).
17. See Debord (2014).
18. See Grande (2015).
19. See Bauman (2001).
20. A wonderfully interesting parallel between the

corporation and the sociopath is developed in the documentary movie *The Corporation*, based on Balkan (2003).

21. See Bailey and Mattei (2013).
22. See Shurtleff and Aoyagi (2014).
23. See Russi (2013).

CHAPTER 10. THE ECOLEGAL REVOLUTION

1. See Macpherson (1962).
2. See the beautiful documentary, based on archival sources, *La zuppa del demonio* (2014), directed by Davide Ferrario.
3. See Capra and Luisi (2014).
4. See Meiksins Wood (2012).
5. See Fardeau and Williamson (2014).
6. For updated data, see Global Footprint Network, www .footprintnetwork.org.
7. See Mattei and Nader (2008).
8. See Orr (1992); Capra (1993, 1996).
9. Orr (2002), 27.
10. Benyus (1997), 2.
11. See, e.g., Hawken, Lovins, and Lovins (1999).
12. See May and Daly (2014).
13. Civil Code, Section 90a, *Bundesgesetzblatt* (Federal Law Gazette), January 2, 2002, last amended on October 1, 2013.
14. On the current path to extend this model in the Trans-Pacific Partnership, see Robert Reich's short video, http://billmoyers .com/2015/02/09/robert-reich -worst-trade-deal-youve-never -heard/.
15. In the United States a notorious 2010 Supreme Court case (*Citizens United v. Federal Election Commission*, 558 U.S. 310) made the larger public aware of this problem.
16. See Horwitz (1994).
17. See Bailey, Farrell, and Mattei (2014).
18. See Zeller (2015).

Glossary of Scientific and Legal Terms

atomism (also *reductionism*). A vision of reality based on the belief that the whole is the algebraic sum of its component parts.

commoning. The social and political activity of taking care of and enjoying something recognized as a common.

commons. A common pool of natural and/or cultural resources (communal institutions), open to all members of society.

descriptive. A term used to describe the way something is, or is done; opposed to *normative.*

ecological literacy (or *ecoliteracy*). Knowledge of the basic principles of organization that ecosystems have evolved to sustain life.

ecology. 1. The science of relationships between the members of an ecological community and their environment. 2. A pattern of relationships that defines the context for a certain phenomenon.

ecology of law (also *ecolegal order*). A legal order that is aimed at nurturing ecological and human communities, and that sees the law as being interdependent with politics, economics, justice, and so on.

feedback loops. A circular arrangement of causally connected elements, in which each element has an effect on the next, until the last "feeds back" the effect into the first element of the cycle.

holism. A vision of reality according to which the whole cannot be reduced to the aggregate of its parts.

individualism. A political vision based on the idea that the individual is the central concern of social life, or organization.

jurisprudence (also *theory of law,* or *philosophy of law*). The theoretical inquiry into legal phenomena.

jurist. A scholar who studies and teaches law.

jus. See under *law.*

law. 1. (in the sense of Latin *jus*) A conceptual framework that abstracts a set of more or less coherent principles and rules from the reality of human relationships. 2. (in the sense of Latin *lex*) A concrete rule (also known as *statute*) to govern human behavior that is enforced by institutions.

law of nature. A short, concise statement or equation summarizing a scientific theory.

legal absolutism (also *legal modernity*). The legal order, triumphant after the French Revolution, based on the principle of ownership as an individual right, guaranteed by the power of the state (*state sovereignty*).

legal positivism. 1. A school of thought claiming that law derives its binding power from a sovereign, regardless of whether it is just, fair, or even rational. 2. A vision of law as a pure entity separate from politics, religion, economics, or morality.

legal rationalism. A version of natural law, originating in Holland after the Reformation, according to which the higher principle that legitimizes law is not God but human reason.

legal system. The orderly combination of particular laws into a whole, according to rational principles.

lex. See under *law*.

modernity. The worldview and practices of the modern era, characterized by rationalism, individualism, professionalism, and the belief in inevitable progress.

natural law. In legal jurisprudence, a school of thought holding that law should be binding only if it is consistent with some validating higher principle.

normative. A term used to describe the way something ought to be, or ought to be done; opposed to *descriptive* (the way something is, or is done).

reductionism. See *atomism*.

rule of law. A Western tradition, according to which a society can be governed according to formal rules that are also binding on those with the actual power of making or interpreting them.

science. An organized body of knowledge acquired through a particular method, known as the scientific method.

sovereignty. The unrestricted power of choice in property or in political matters.

sustainability. The characteristic of a community designed in such a way that its ways of life do not interfere with nature's inherent ability to sustain life.

systems thinking (or *systemic thinking*). Thinking in terms of relationships, patterns, and context.

Bibliography

Alford, W. 1995. *To Steal a Book Is an Elegant Offence: Intellectual Property Law in Chinese Civilization*. Stanford, Calif.: Stanford University Press.

Arendt, Hannah. 2006. *Eichman in Jerusalem: A Report on the Banality of Evil*. New York: Penguin Books. First published in 1963.

Bailey, S., G. Farrell, and U. Mattei. 2014. *Protecting Future Generations through Commons*. Trends in Social Cohesion 26. Strasbourg: Council of Europe.

Bailey, S., and U. Mattei. 2013. "Social Movements as Constituent Power: The Italian Struggle for the Commons." *Indiana Journal of Global Legal Studies* 20:930.

Baker, J. H. 2002. *An Introduction to English Legal History*. 4th ed. London: Butterworth Lexis Nexis.

Balkan, J. 2003. *The Corporation: The Pathological Pursuit of Profit and Power*. New York: Free Press.

Barnes, P. 2006. *Capitalism 3.0: A Guide to Reclaiming the Commons*. San Francisco: Berrett-Koehler.

Barron, Anne, et al. 2002. *Introduction to Jurisprudence and Legal Theory: Commentary and Materials*. Oxford: Oxford University Press.

Bauman, Z. 2001. *Community: Seeking Security in an Unsecure World*. Boston: Polity Press.

Benyus, Janine. 1997. *Biomimicry*. New York: Morrow.

Berlin, I. 2013. *The Roots of Romanticism*. Princeton, N.J.: Princeton University Press.

Berman, H. 1985. *Law and Revolution: The Formation of the Western Legal Tradition*. Cambridge, Mass.: Harvard University Press.

Black, Stephanie, producer and director. 2001. *Life and Debt* (documentary film). Tuff Gong Pictures.

Blaug, M. 1996. *Economic Theory in Retrospect*. 5th ed. Cambridge: Cambridge University Press.

Bollier, D. 2014. *Think Like a Commoner: A Short Introduction to the Life of the Commons*. Gabriola Island, Canada: New Society Publishers.

Bollier, D., and S. Helfrich, eds. 2012. *The Wealth of the Commons: A World beyond Market and State*. The Commons Strategies Group. Amherst, Mass.: Levellers Press.

Boyle, J. 2003. "The Second Enclosure Movement and the Construction of the Public Domain." *Law and Contemporary Problems* 66:33.

Brown, Lester. 1981. *Building a Sustainable Society*. New York: Norton.

———. 2009. *Plan B. Mobilizing to Save Civilization*. New York: Earth Policy Institute, Norton.

Buchanan, James, and Gordon Tullock. 2004. *The Calculus of Consent: Logical Foundations of Constitutional Democracy*. Indianapolis, Ind.: Liberty Fund.

Buckland, W. W. 1936. *Roman Law and the Common Law: A Comparison in Outline*. Cambridge: Cambridge University Press.

———. 1963. *A Textbook of Roman Law: From Augustus to Justinian*. 3rd ed. Reviewed by Peter Stein. Cambridge: Cambridge University Press.

Capra, Fritjof. 1975. *The Tao of Physics*. Boston: Shambhala.

———, ed. 1993. *Guide to Ecoliteracy*. Berkeley, Calif.: Center for Ecoliteracy.

———. 1996. *The Web of Life*. New York: Anchor/Doubleday.

———. 2002. *The Hidden Connections*. New York: Doubleday.

———. 2007. *The Science of Leonardo*. New York: Doubleday.

———. 2013. *Learning from Leonardo*. San Francisco: Berrett-Koehler.

Capra, Fritjof, and Pier Luigi Luisi. 2014. *The Systems View of Life: A Unifying Vision*. Cambridge: Cambridge University Press.

Cardozo, Benjamin Nathan. 1921. *The Nature of the Judicial Process*. New Haven, Conn.: Yale University Press.

Cassi, A. A. 2007. *Ultramar: L'invenzione europea del Nuovo Mondo* [Ultramar: The European invention of the New World]. Bari and Rome: Laterza.

Castells, Manuel. 1996. *The Information Age*. Vol. 1: *The Rise of the Network Society*. Malden, Mass.: Blackwell.

———. 1998. *The Information Age*. Vol. 3: *End of Millennium*. Malden, Mass.: Blackwell.

Collum, Ed, et al. 2012. *Equal Time, Equal Value: Community Currencies and Time Banking in the US*. Farnham, UK: Ashgate.

Daston, Lorraine, and Michael Stolleis, eds. 2008. *Natural Law and Laws of Nature in Early Modern Europe*. Farnham, UK: Ashgate.

Dawson, J. P. 1983. *The Oracles of the Law*. Ann Arbor: University of Michigan.

Debord, G. 2014. *The Society of the Spectacle*. Berkeley, Calif.: Bureau of Public Secrets.

Dezalay, I., and B. Garth. 1998. *Dealing in Virtue: International Commercial Arbitration and the Construction of a Transnational Legal Order*. Chicago: University of Chicago Press.

Dicker, Georges. 2013. *Descartes: An Analytical and Historical Introduction*. 2nd ed. Oxford: Oxford University Press.

Dietze, G. 1995. *In Defense of Property*. Lanham, Md.: University Press of America.

Dworkin, R. 2013. *Taking Rights Seriously*. London: Bloomsbury Academic.

Eiseley, Loren. 1961. *Darwin's Century: Evolution and the Man Who Discovered It*. New York: Anchor Books.

Ellis, J. J. 2002. *Founding Brothers: The Revolutionary Generation*. London: Vintage Books.

Ely, J. W. 2008. *The Guardian of Every Other Right: A Constitutional History of Property Rights*. 3rd ed. Oxford: Oxford University Press.

Engels, Friedrich. 1972. *The Origin of the Family, Private Property and the State*. New York: International Books.

Fardeau, Jean-Marie, and Hugh Williamson. 2014. "Letter to the French Minister of Interior: Regarding the Death of Rémi Fraisse and the Use of Force during Demonstrations." Human Rights Watch. November 19. http://www.hrw.org/news/2014/11/19/letter-french-minister-interior.

Foucault, Michel. 1975. *Discipline and Punish: The Birth of the Prison*. London: Vintage Books.

Friedman, L. M. 2010. *A History of American Law*. Rev. ed. New York: Simon & Schuster.

Galbraith, John Kenneth. 1958. *The Affluent Society*. New York and Toronto: Mentor Books.

Galeano, E. 1973. *Open Veins of Latin America: Five Centuries of Pillage of a Continent*. New York: Monthly Review Press.

Garnsey, P. 2007. *Thinking about Property: From Antiquity to the Age of Revolution*. Cambridge: Cambridge University Press.

Giardini, Federica, Ugo Mattei, and Rafael Spregelburd. 2012. *Teatro Valle occupato: La rivolta culturale dei beni comuni* [Teatro Valle occupied: The cultural revolt of the commons]. Rome: DeriveApprodi.

Gilmore, G. 2014. *The Ages of American Law*. 2nd ed. New Haven, Conn.: Yale University Press.

Gonzales, V., and R. Philips. 2014. *Cooperatives and Community Development*. Abingdon, U.K.: Routledge.

Gordley, James. 1990. *The Philosophical Origins of Modern Contract Doctrine*. Oxford: Oxford University Press.

———. 2013. *The Jurists: A Critical History*. Oxford: Oxford University Press.

Grande, E. 2015. "I Do It for Myself!: The Dark Side of Women's Rights." In *Humanitarianism Inc.*, edited by A. De Lauri. London: I. B. Tauris.

Grossi, Paolo. 1975. *Un altro modo di possedere* [Another way to possess]. Milan: Giuffré.

———. 2006. *L'ordine giuridico medievale* [The medieval legal order]. Bari and Roma: Laterza.

———. 2010. *A History of European Law*. Malden, Mass.: Blackwell-Wiley.

Haakonssen, Knud. 1996. *Natural Law and Moral Philosophy: From Grotius to the Scottish Enlightenment*. Cambridge, UK: Cambridge University Press.

Hardin, Garrett. 1968. "The Tragedy of the Commons." *Science* 162, no. 3859: 1243–1248.

Hardt, Michael, and Antonio Negri. 2000. *Empire*. Cambridge, Mass.: Harvard University Press.

———. 2009. *Commonwealth*. Cambridge, Mass.: Harvard University Press.

Harper, D. 2012. *The Community Land Trusts: Affordable Access to Land and Housing*. New York: UN-Habitat.

Hart, H. L. A. 2012. *The Concept of Law*. 3rd ed. Oxford: Clarendon Press.

Hawken, Paul. 2010. *The Ecology of Commerce: A Declaration of Sustainability*. Rev. ed. New York: Harper Business, 2010.

Hawken, Paul, Amory Lovins, and Hunter Lovins. 1999. *Natural Capitalism*. New York: Little, Brown.

Held, David, and Anthony McGrew. 2003. *The Global Transformations Reader*. 2nd ed. Hoboken, N.J.: Wiley.

Hertz, Noreena. 2001. *The Silent Takeover: Global Capitalism and the Death of Democracy*. New York: Harper Business.

Honoré, Toni. 1962. *Gaius*. Oxford: Clarendon Press.

Horwitz, Morton. 1994. *The Transformation of American Law, 1870–1960*. New York: Oxford University Press.

Hume, David. (1740) 2000. *Treatise of Human Nature*. Oxford: Oxford Philosophical Press.

Kelly, Marjorie. 2001. *The Divine Right of Capital: Dethroning the Corporate Aristocracy*. San Francisco: Berrett-Koehler.

———. 2012. *Owning Our Future: The Emerging Ownership Revolution*. San Francisco: Berrett-Koehler.

Kennedy, D. 2006. "Three Globalizations of Law and Legal Thought, 1850–2000." In *The New Law and Economic Development*, edited by D. Trubeck and A. Santos. New York: Cambridge University Press.

Klein, Naomi. 2007. *The Shock Doctrine: The Rise of Disaster Capitalism*. New York: Metropolitan Books.

———. 2014. *This Changes Everything*. New York: Simon & Schuster.

Kroft, Steve. 2008. "The Bet That Blew Up Wall Street." CBS *Sixty Minutes*, October 16.

Kuhn, Thomas S. 1996. *The Structure of Scientific Revolutions*. Chicago: University of Chicago Press.

Kuttner, Robert. 2010. *A Presidency in Peril: The Inside Story of Obama's Promise, Wall Street's Power, and the Struggle to Control Our Economic Future*. Chelsea, U.K.: Green Publishing.

Levy, Ernst. 1951. *West Roman Vulgar Law: The Law of Property*. Memoirs of the American Philosophical Society 29. Philadelphia: American Philosophical Society.

Linebaugh, Peter. 2008. *The Magna Carta Manifesto: Liberties and Commons for All*. Berkeley: University of California Press.

Llewellyn, Karl. 2012. *The Bramble Bush: On Our Law and Its Study*. New Orleans: Quid Pro Books.

Lucarelli, Stefano, and Giorgio Lunghini. 2012. *The Resistible Rise of Mainstream Economics: The Dominant Theory and the Alternative Economic Theories*. Bergamo, Italy: Bergamo University Press.

Lupoi, Maurizio. 2006. *The Origins of the European Legal Order*. Translated by Adrian Belton. Cambridge, U.K.: Cambridge University Press.

Macpherson, C. B. 1962. *The Political Theory of Possessive Individualism: Hobbes to Locke*. Oxford: Clarendon Press.

Magnani, Esteban. 2009. *The Silent Change: Recovered Businesses in Argentina*. Buenos Aires: Teseo.

Mallaby, Sebastian. 2010. *More Money Than God: Hedge Funds and the Making of a New Elite*. London: Bloomsbury.

Mander, Jerry. 2012. *The Capitalism Papers*. Berkeley, Calif.: Counterpoint.

Mander, Jerry, and Edward Goldsmith, eds. 1996. *The Case against the Global Economy*. San Francisco: Sierra Club Books.

Marx, Karl. (1867) 1992. *Capital: A Critique of Political Economy*. Vol. 1. London: Penguin Classics.

Mattei, Ugo. 1997. *Comparative Law and Economics*. Ann Arbor: University of Michigan Press.

———. 2000. *Basic Principles of Property Law: A Comparative Legal and Economic Introduction*. Westport, Conn.: Greenwood.

———. 2011. *Beni comuni: Un manifesto* [Common goods: A manifesto]. 9th ed. Rome: Laterza. (Spanish translation, *Bienes comunes: Un manifesto*, Madrid, Editorial Trotta, 2013).

Mattei, Ugo, and Laura Nader. 2008. *Plunder: When the Rule of Law Is Illegal*. Malden, Mass.: Blackwell.

Maturana, Humberto, and Francisco Varela. 1987. *The Tree of Knowledge*. Boston: Shambhala.

May, J. R., and E. Daly. 2014. *Environmental Constitutionalism*. Cambridge, U.K.: Cambridge University Press.

Meadows, Donella, et al. 1972. *The Limits to Growth*. New York: Universe Books.

Meiksins Wood, Ellen. 2012. *Liberty and Property: A Social History of Western Political Thought from the Renaissance to Enlightenment*. London and New York: Verso.

Merchant, Carolyn. 1990. *The Death of Nature: Women, Ecology, and the Scientific Revolution*. San Francisco: Harper.

Milsom, S. F. C. 1985. *Studies in the History of the Common Law*. London: Hambledon Press.

Mofid, Kamran, and Steve Szeghi. 2010. "Economics in Crisis: What Do We Tell the Students?" Share the World's Resources, www.stwr.org.

More, Thomas. (1523) 2010. *Utopia*. Red Wing, Minn.: Cricket House Books.

Nader, Laura. 1990. *Harmony Ideology: Justice and Control in a Zapotec Mountain Village*. Stanford, Calif.: Stanford University Press.

———. 2005. *The Life of the Law: Anthropological Projects*. Berkeley: University of California Press.

———. 2014. *Naked Science: Anthropological Inquiry into Boundaries, Power, and Knowledge*. London and New York: Routledge.

Noble, David F. 2013. *America by Design: Science, Technology, and the Rise of Corporate Capitalism*. New York: Knopf.

Oakley, Francis. 2005. *Natural Law, Laws of Nature, Natural Rights: Continuity and Discontinuity in the History of Ideas*. New York: Continuum.

Orr, David. 1992. *Ecological Literacy*. Albany: State University of New York Press.

———. 2002. *The Nature of Design*. New York: Oxford University Press.

Ostrom, Elinor. 1990. *Governing the Commons: The Evolution of Institutions for Collective Action*. Cambridge: Cambridge University Press.

Penalver, Eduardo M., and Sonia K. Katyal. 2010. *Property Outlaws: How Pirates, Squatters, and Protesters Improve the Law of Ownership*. New Haven, Conn.: Yale University Press.

Perkins, John. 2004. *Confessions of an Economic Hit Man*. San Francisco: Berrett-Koehler.

Piketty, Thomas. 2014. *Capital in the Twenty-First Century*. Translated by Arthur Goldhammer. Cambridge, Mass.: Harvard University Press.

Plucknett, T. F. T. 2001. *A Concise History of the Common Law*. 5th ed. Union, N.J.: The Law Book Exchange.

Polanyi, Karl. 1949. *The Great Transformation: The Political and Economic Origins of Our Time*. Boston: Beacon.

Posner, Richard A. 2014. *Economic Analysis of Law*. 9th ed. New York: Wolters Kluwer.

Pound, Roscoe. 1910. "Law in Books and Law in Action: Historical Cases of Divergence between Nominal and Actual Law." *American Law Review* 44:12–36.

———. 2012. *Mechanical Jurisprudence*. General Books. Originally published in *Columbia Law Review* 8, no. 8 (December 1908): 605–623.

Prigogine, Ilya, and Isabelle Stengers. 1984. *Order out of Chaos*. New York: Bantam.

Reimann, Mathias, et al. 2013. *Transnational Law: Cases and Materials*. St. Paul, Minn.: West Academic.

Richards, Robert. 2002. *The Romantic Conception of Life*. Chicago: University of Chicago Press.

Riesman, D. 2001. *The Lonely Crowd*. Revised and abridged edition. New Haven, Conn.: Yale University Press.

Robbins, Lionel. 1998. *A History of Economic Thought: The LSE Lectures*. Edited by S. G. Medema and W. J. Samuels. Princeton, N.J.: Princeton University Press.

Rodis-Lewis, Geneviève. 1978. "Limitations of the Mechanical Model in the Cartesian Conception of the Organism." In *Descartes*, edited by Michael Hooker. Baltimore: Johns Hopkins University Press.

Rodotà, S. 2013. *Il terribile diritto: Studi sulla proprietà private e sui beni comuni* [The terrible right: Studies on private property and the commons]. Bologna: Il Mulino.

Ross, A. 2013. *Creditocracy and the Case for Debt Refusal*. New York and London: OR Books.

Rowe, J. 2013. *Our Common Wealth*. Edited by P. Barnes. San Francisco: Berrett-Koehler.

Roy, Tirthankar. 2012. *The East India Company: The World's Most Powerful Corporation*. London: Penguin.

Russi, L. 2013. *Hungry Capital: The Financialization of Food*. London: John Hunt Publishing.

Shurtleff, William, and Akiko Aoyagi. 2014. *History of Meat Alternatives, 965 CE –2014*. Lafayette, Calif.: Soyinfo Center.

Siegle, Lucy. 2014. *We Are What We Wear: Unravelling Fast Fashion and the Collapse of Rana Plaza*. London: Guardian Books.

Stein, P. 2009. *Legal Evolution: The Story of an Idea*. Cambridge: Cambridge University Press.

Stout, Lynn. 2012. *The Shareholder Value Myth: How Putting Shareholders First Harms Investors, Corporations, and the Public*. San Francisco: Berrett-Koehler.

Swartz, B. 1998. *The Code Napoleon and the Common Law World*. Union, N.J.: The Law Book Exchange.

Tigar, Michael. 2005. *Law and the Rise of Capitalism*. 2nd edition with Madeleine Levy. Delhi: AAKAR.

Tönnies, Ferdinand. 2001. *Community and Civil Society*. Cambridge: Cambridge University Press.

Twining, William. 2009. *General Jurisprudence: Understanding Law from a Global Perspective*. Cambridge: Cambridge University Press.

Unger, R. 1976. *Knowledge and Politics*. New York: Simon & Schuster.

Valguarnera, F. 2014. *Accesso alla natura tra ideologia e diritto* [Access to nature between ideology and law]. 2nd ed. Turin: Giappichelli.

Van Caenegem, R. C. 1993. *Judges, Legislators, and Professors: Chapters in European Legal History*. Cambridge: Cambridge University Press.

Watson, Alan. 1968. *The Law of Property in the Later Roman Republic*. Oxford: Clarendon Press.

———. 1995. *The Spirit of Roman Law*. Athens: University of Georgia Press.

Whitman, J. Q. 1990. *The Legacy of Roman Law in the German Romantic Era: Historical Vision and Legal Change*. Princeton, N.J.: Princeton University Press.

Wieacker, Franz. 1995. *A History of Private Law in Europe*. Oxford: Clarendon Press.

Wildlife Society. 2010. *The Public Trust Doctrine: Implications for Wildlife Management and Conservation in the United States and Canada*. Worthy Shorts.

World Commission on Environment and Development. 1987. *Our Common Future*. Oxford: Oxford University Press.

Wrights, C. 2014. *Workers Cooperatives and Revolution: History and Possibilities in the United States.* Bobklocker.

Zeller, Tom, Jr. 2015. "Why Teenagers Are Suing States over Climate Change." *Forbes*, April 8, http://www.forbes.com/sites /tomzeller/2015/04/08/why-teenagers-are-suing-states-over -climate-change/.

Acknowledgments

We wish to thank Carlton Jones for introducing us to each other on the tennis court, and Shauna Marshall, former academic dean at Hastings College of the Law, for giving us the opportunity to explore our ideas in two graduate seminars in 2009 and 2010.

We are very grateful to David Faigman, Radhicka Rao, Talha Sayed, and Tarek Milleron for helpful comments and suggestions; and to Steve Piersanti, Jeevan Sivasubramaniam, and the entire Berrett-Koehler team for their enthusiastic support. Our special thanks go to Todd Manza for his superb editing of an unwieldy first draft, and we are grateful to Elizabeth Hawk for her help in the cover design.

Ugo Mattei would like to express his gratitude to the many comrades who, in the struggle for the commons, continue to show that another world is possible. Special thanks to Elisabetta, Clara, Greta, and Adam Mattei.

Index

About the Authors

FRITJOF CAPRA, Ph.D., physicist
and systems theorist, is a
founding director of the Center for Ecoliteracy in Berkeley,
California, which is dedicated
to promoting ecology and
systems thinking in primary
and secondary education.
He is a fellow of Schumacher
College, an international
center for ecological studies
in the United Kingdom, and
serves on the Council of Earth
Charter International.

AUTHOR PHOTO: BASSO CANNARSA

After receiving his Ph.D. in theoretical physics from the University of Vienna in 1966, Capra did research in particle physics at
the University of Paris (1966–1968), the University of California at
Santa Cruz (1968–1970), the Stanford Linear Accelerator Center
(1970), Imperial College, University of London (1971–1974), and
the Lawrence Berkeley Laboratory at the University of California
(1975–1988).

In addition to his research in physics and systems theory,
Capra has been engaged in a systematic examination of the philosophical and social implications of contemporary science for the
past forty years. His books on this subject have been acclaimed
internationally, and he has lectured widely to lay and professional
audiences in Europe, Asia, and North and South America.

Capra is the author of several international bestsellers, including *The Tao of Physics* (1975), *The Turning Point* (1982), *The Web of Life* (1996), *The Hidden Connections* (2002), *The Science of Leonardo* (2007), and *Learning from Leonardo* (2013). He is coauthor, with Pier Luigi Luisi, of the multidisciplinary textbook *The Systems View of Life: A Unifying Vision* (2014). He has been the focus of more than sixty television interviews, documentaries, and talk shows in Europe, the United States, Brazil, Argentina, and Japan, and has been featured in major newspapers and magazines internationally. He was the first subject of the BBC's documentary series *Beautiful Minds* (2002).

Capra holds an Honorary Doctor of Science degree from the University of Plymouth and is the recipient of many other awards, including the Gold Medal of the UK Systems Society, the Neil Postman Award for Career Achievement in Public Intellectual Activity from the Media Ecology Association, the Medal of the Presidency of the Italian Republic, the Leonardo da Vinci Medallion of Honor from the University of Advancing Technology in Tempe, Arizona, the Bioneers Award, the New Dimensions Broadcaster Award, the American Book Award, and the Gold IndieFab Award from *Foreword Reviews*.

Fritjof Capra lives in Berkeley with his wife and daughter. www.fritjofcapra.net

UGO MATTEI is a chaired professor of law at Hastings College of the Law, San Francisco, and at the University of Turin, Italy.

From 2011 to 2014 he served as president of the Aqueduct of Naples, the first Italian company governed according to participatory commons bylaws, which provides drinking water to one of the largest port metropolises of the South Mediterranean. He served as a

deputy mayor of Chieri, a medieval town in the northern region of Piedmont, Italy, with a population of 37,000.

He has written many books, including the standard textbooks of property law and of Anglo-American law for Italian students. His bestselling Italian book, *Beni comuni: Un manifesto*, published in 2011, has reached its ninth edition and is the standard reference for the Italian commons movement. His book *Plunder*, published in 2008 with anthropologist Laura Nader, has been translated into six languages.

In 2008 he funded the International University College of Turin, a graduate institution devoted to providing free interdisciplinary education on the institutions of global capitalism.

In 2011 Mattei masterminded a nationwide referendum against the privatization of water that obtained an overwhelming success, with more than 27 million votes.

Mattei is a member of the Supreme Court Bar of Italy, a fellow of the European Law Institute, and a member of the International Academy of Comparative Law.

Berrett–Koehler
Publishers

Berrett-Koehler is an independent publisher dedicated to an ambitious mission: *connecting people and ideas to create a world that works for all.*

We believe that to truly create a better world, action is needed at all levels—individual, organizational, and societal. At the individual level, our publications help people align their lives with their values and with their aspirations for a better world. At the organizational level, our publications promote progressive leadership and management practices, socially responsible approaches to business, and humane and effective organizations. At the societal level, our publications advance social and economic justice, shared prosperity, sustainability, and new solutions to national and global issues.

A major theme of our publications is "Opening Up New Space." Berrett-Koehler titles challenge conventional thinking, introduce new ideas, and foster positive change. Their common quest is changing the underlying beliefs, mindsets, institutions, and structures that keep generating the same cycles of problems, no matter who our leaders are or what improvement programs we adopt.

We strive to practice what we preach—to operate our publishing company in line with the ideas in our books. At the core of our approach is stewardship, which we define as a deep sense of responsibility to administer the company for the benefit of all of our "stakeholder" groups: authors, customers, employees, investors, service providers, and the communities and environment around us.

We are grateful to the thousands of readers, authors, and other friends of the company who consider themselves to be part of the "BK Community." We hope that you, too, will join us in our mission.

A BK Currents Book

This book is part of our BK Currents series. BK Currents books advance social and economic justice by exploring the critical intersections between business and society. Offering a unique combination of thoughtful analysis and progressive alternatives, BK Currents books promote positive change at the national and global levels. To find out more, visit **www.bkconnection.com**.

Berrett–Koehler
Publishers

Connecting people and ideas
to create a world that works for all

Dear Reader,

Thank you for picking up this book and joining our worldwide community of Berrett-Koehler readers. We share ideas that bring positive change into people's lives, organizations, and society.

To welcome you, we'd like to offer you a free e-book. You can pick from among twelve of our bestselling books by entering the promotional code **BKP92E** here: http://www.bkconnection.com/welcome.

When you claim your free e-book, we'll also send you a copy of our e-newsletter, the *BK Communiqué*. Although you're free to unsubscribe, there are many benefits to sticking around. In every issue of our newsletter you'll find

- A free e-book
- Tips from famous authors
- Discounts on spotlight titles
- Hilarious insider publishing news
- A chance to win a prize for answering a riddle

Best of all, our readers tell us, "Your newsletter is the only one I actually read." So claim your gift today, and please stay in touch!

Sincerely,

Charlotte Ashlock
Steward of the BK Website

Questions? Comments? Contact me at bkcommunity@bkpub.com.

MIX
Paper from
responsible sources
FSC® C002589

Certified

Corporation
bcorporation.net